The German Catastrophe

REFLECTIONS AND RECOLLECTIONS

BY

FRIEDRICH MEINECKE

TRANSLATED BY

SIDNEY B. FAY

BEACON PRESS   BOSTON

First published in 1950 by Harvard University Press
Copyright 1950 by the President and Fellows of Harvard College
First published as a Beacon Paperback in 1963
by arrangement with the original publisher
All rights reserved
Printed in the United States of America
Beacon Press books are published under the auspices
of the Unitarian Universalist Association

International Standard Book Number: 0–8070–5667–7

15   14   13   12   11   10   9

Friedrich Meinecke (1862-1954) was one of the most revered and distinguished of recent German historians. Gentle in manner but vigorous in mind, small in stature and somewhat frail in body, he remained mentally active until his death at the age of ninety-two. His long span of life enabled him to observe and reflect upon the tragic cycle of Germany's rise and fall as a great power. As a boy he watched the return of the victorious German troops from France in 1871, and admired the skill with which Bismark established the long-desired unification of his country. As a young archivist and later as professor he observed Germany's tremendous strides in industrial and commercial expansion, the growth of the socialist masses, and the international rivalries which culminated in war and the humiliating Versailles Treaty. Under the Weimar Republic he was dismaycd at the irresponsibility of the wrangling political factions and saw with foreboding the gathering strength of the Nazis. With Hitler's seizure of power in 1933, Meinecke was forthwith dismissed from the position which he had filled with distinction for forty years as editor of the *Historische Zeitschrift,* the leading journal of German historical scholarship. During World War II the aged scholar suffered spiritual agony and physical hardship. He was the personal friend of General Beck and had some inkling of plans to rid the country of Hitler, but took no active part in them.

As a humane liberal, profoundly opposed to Hitler's brutal suppression of personal freedom, fraudulent promises, racial persecution and dangerous megalomania, Meinecke might at any time have escaped by fleeing abroad. But like so many other patriotic Germans, he believed he could do more for his country by staying at home, hastening the inevitable downfall of Hitler, and by building up a new Germany based upon her better and older traditions. This little book, written at the time of Germany's utter defeat and deepest despair, was the result of the latter aim.

One of the great merits of *Die Deutsche Katastrophe* (Wiesbaden, 1946; English translation, Harvard University Press, 1950) is its comparative brevity. In contrast to some of the bulky volumes mentioned below, it can be easily read in an evening. Considering that Professor Meinecke deals with German development during more than a hundred years, from the era of Goethe's classical liberalism to the downfall of the Nazi tyranny, this brevity is remarkable. It is possible because Meinecke makes no attempt to give a detailed narrative of familiar events, but confines himself to a deft, penetrating and condensed indication of political, moral and psychological trends. He points out when and where the German people and their rulers followed the wrong turn in the road. He touches on highly important controversial questions. How far were Germany's disasters attributable to her geographical situation, to her national characteristics, to chance events, or to "fate"? Why did the attempt to harmonize the two great forces of the age — nationalism and socialism (which succeeded in the case of the British Labor Party) fail in Germany, the case of Friedrich Naumann's good pre-1914 national socialism, thus leaving the path open for Hitler's disasterous National Socialism? To what extent was totalitarianism a peculiar German phenomenon rather than an aspect of a general European development?

Meinecke's poignant self-searching revelation of his own spiritual and intellectual convictions as to his country's successes, errors and misfortunes is also significant for the student of today. His analysis affords a valuable clue to the extraordinary evolution of Western Germany during the past decade and a half — not, to be sure, to its almost miraculous material recovery, but to its spiritual and intellectual vigor and to the reorientation of its political goals. At the moment when Germany was utterly crushed and shorn of her eastern lands, he still had faith that his country would be able to return to its better traditions, regain its cultural heritage, and even play a cosmopolitan role among the powers of western Europe. He envisaged Germany as becoming eventually a member of a European Federation assuming a worthy but modest role similar to that of Holland and Sweden which had once been great powers in the world. He did not foresee, however, that a West German Federal Republic, guided by the wise moderation and Christian spirit of Konrad Adenauer, would become the trusted ally of recent enemies and the leading member of a new economic community.

Meinecke's faith in Germany's future, his candid exposure of her anachronistic militarism, imperialism and fraudulent Nazism, and his eloquent emphasis on cultural ideals exerted a beneficent influence on Germany's postwar youth. It was eminently appropriate, shortly after the publication of his book, that he was chosen Rector of the New Berlin University, which now flourishes in the free western sector of the city while the old university languishes in the Communist sector.

For present-day readers, Meinecke's analysis of the German catastrophe has a certain significance because it throws a warning light on contemporary problems and dangers in the nuclear world of today. For the world is still faced with the same questions which he considers in Germany's case. To what extent is the nation-state justified in employing practices which would not be morally permissible for the individual? It is a question that has been continually argued since the days of Machiavelli, and one to which Meinecke himself devoted a whole volume shortly after World War I (*Die Idee der Staatsräson in der Neueren Geschichte,* 1924; 7th edition 1928; new edition by Walther Hofer, 1957). There are still the fears, suspicions and terrible financial burdens caused by mounting armaments. We still suffer from the propagandist poisoning of public opinion by the press and the radio. There are still the dangers of pressure of the military and of the big industrial interests upon the civilian authorities. President Eisenhower, in his memorable valedictory address to the nation, called attention to the "conjunction of an immense military establishment and a large arms industry." He solemnly warned of the dangerous influence that such a "military-industrial complex" might exert.

Many of the best, or at least most widely read, books which seek to explain Germany and the Nazi regime emphasize some one particular factor, or concentrate upon Hitler's personality and Satanic influence, or enter into great detail and cover only a short period of time. Thus, for instance, Erich Fromm, in *Escape from Freedom*, emphasizes submission to Hitler and Nazism as a psychological consequence of the sadist-masochist character of the German people. Franz Neumann, in *Behemoth*, gave an admirable detailed description of Nazi totalitarian organization and economic methods as they existed in 1942. J. W. Wheeler-Bennett, Gordon Craig and Gerhard Ritter, each in his own way, have supplied thorough historical accounts of the disciplined technical efficiency but fatal political narrowness of vision of the Prussian General Staff. William L. Shirer, making large use of the evidence against the Nazis collected for the Nuremberg trials, devotes *The Rise and Fall of the Third Reich* mainly to Hitler's personality. He gives a dramatic narrative of the steps by which Hitler rose to power, launched war, escaped plots to get rid of him, and plunged Germany, along with himself, into the abyss of self-destruction. A. J. P. Taylor, an Englishman, offers a picture of the European diplomacy between the two wars in his too facile and brilliantly short study, *The Origins of the Second World War*. He rightly points out the effects of the Versailles Treaty and the British and French mistakes, which Hitler turned to his own advantage. But Taylor then turns his picture absurdly askew by virtually ignoring *Mein Kampf*, Hitler's determined preparations for the military seizure of *Lebensraum*, and his tricky provocations before the swallowing of Austria and Czechoslovakia. As a result, Taylor's one-sided account leaves the reader with the erroneous impression that it was not Hitler, but the English and the French who are chiefly to blame for the Second World War. K. D. Bracher and two collaborators published in 1960 a monumental thousand-page study *(Die nationalsozialistische Machtergreifung . . . 1933-1934)* which analyzed meticulously Hitler's "pseudo-legal" seizure and consolidation of power. It describes admirably and in minute detail all the weapons of *Gleichschaltung* — social, economic, psychological and military — by which the Nazis tricked and terrorized the different elements in the population into submission to the charismatic leader. It is perhaps the most authoritative analysis that has yet been written, but as its title indicates, it covers only the first two years of the Nazi regime. In comparison with such diverse books, and a multitude of others, each with the defects of its qualities, Professor Meinecke's brief but comprehensive little book has certain advantages of its own. It scans a whole century, avoids falling into excessive detail or overemphasis of any one aspect of the subject, and thus subtly achieves a kind of introductory birds-eye view of the German disaster. It sums up the mature reflections and revised opinions of an old man contemplating the ruin. It seeks neither to justify nor to condemn, but to understand. And, like a good historian, Meinecke sees things not purely white or black, but as the merging of lighter and darker shades in the gray web of history.

To give an adequate rendering into English of Professor Meinecke's condensed style, poetic metaphors, and nuances of thought is not easy. I have tried to render his meaning as faithfully as possible without being too slavishly literal. A word of explanation, perhaps, should be given about two words, *culture* and *civilization*. When Germans speak of Western *culture,* they have in mind the art, music, philosophy, science, religion, etc., of Greece, Rome, the Renaissance, and modern times, but they do not include the more material things of life. When they say that we in America have an advanced *civilization,* they are not thinking so much of the things just mentioned as *culture,* but of the fact that we have autos, radios and efficient mass production of all sorts of mechanical appliances. This explains what Professor Meinecke means when he speaks of a stage in which culture flattens or shallows out into civilization.

Cambridge, Mass.   Sidney B. Fay
                                    Professor Emeritus of European
                                    History, Harvard University

CONTENTS

AUTHOR'S PREFACE

Will one ever fully understand the monstrous experiences which fell to our lot in the twelve years of the Third Reich? We have lived through them, but up to now we — every one of us without exception — have understood them only incompletely. This or that side of our fate, to be sure, has stood before our eyes, often in glaring light, apparently free from any uncertainty. But who is able to explain completely how it all fits together and how it was interwoven with deeper causes; how the boundless illusions to which so many succumbed in the first years of the Third Reich necessarily changed into the boundless disillusionment and collapse of the final years? German history is rich in difficult riddles and unfortunate turns. But for our comprehension the riddle that confronts us today and the catastrophe through which we are now living surpass all previous occurrences of similar kind.

The reflections which we have gathered together are only a piece of the picture, only spade work for future efforts to understand more profoundly our fate. Out of the abundance of experiences only certain problems of inner and more permanent significance will be selected. I pass over in silence, for instance, all Hitler's political successes in the years before the outbreak of the Second World War — they have all vanished away into nothingness. Many a German reader who agreed with me in condemning Hitlerism will find too severe my criticism of the German bourgeoisie and Prussian-German militarism, and will want to plead "extenuating circumstances" for both. As if I had not always weighed such considerations in my mind! In the present situation, however, it seemed to me more important and more urgent to mind my own business. And so, for compelling reasons, I must refrain from reflecting on certain problems of the future of the world situation. The subtler reasons why what is said today can be only fragmentary lie in the spiritual and intellectual shocks to which all contemporaries and witnesses of this frightful period have been subjected — not only those immediately stricken but also those throughout the world who were only looking on. These shocks inevitably clouded every judgment, no matter how hard one might try to see things clearly and objectively. Moreover, there is the lack of good and reliable source material.

The need, however, for a fuller understanding is now here, and justifies even incomplete attempts to enlarge our understanding. These attempts in turn may hope to contribute to later efforts something which no investigation resting on merely written sources can ever offer — the essence of the atmosphere of the period in which our fate was fulfilled, and of which one must be aware in order fully to understand this fate.

I have therefore felt justified in relating or mentioning much that still lacks critical attestation; for example, characteristic Hitler sayings that were told to me by trustworthy people. Should one let these sayings fall into oblivion? I have also noted down remarks which seemed to me to be in harmony with the nature of the man. Later criticism can then either confirm or reject them on the basis of fuller and more reliable material.

The reflections offered here are not simply the fruit of the final catastrophe. From the beginning I regarded Hitler's seizure of power as one of the very greatest misfortunes for Germany and have ever and again tested and completed my belief in countless conversations with contemporaries capable of judgment. It is therefore the intellectual and political opposition to Hitler which speaks here, as well as in the recollections which are interwoven with the reflections. I ought not to allow to fall into oblivion what I heard in the exchange of views with Groener, Brüning, Beck, and others, in so far as it was historically significant.

While writing, I was handicapped in many ways by trouble with my eyes, and, aside from some reading notes, I had to depend almost wholly upon my memory. I hope the reader will make allowance for the resulting deficiencies. And may my jottings, limited as their value can only be today, contribute to the beginning of a new existence — to be sure a bowed-down, but a spiritually purer, existence. May they strengthen the determination to turn what remains of our own strength toward preserving what remains of Germany's people and culture.

1 THE TWO WAVES OF THE AGE

The question of the deeper causes of the frightful catastrophe which burst upon Germany will still occupy the coming centuries — provided these centuries are indeed still able and inclined to ponder problems of this kind. But then the question of the German catastrophe broadens at the same time to a question which extends beyond Germany to the destiny of the West in general. Hitler's National Socialism, which brought us directly to this abyss, is not a phenomenon deriving from merely German evolutionary forces, but has also certain analogies and precedents in the authoritarian systems of neighboring countries, however horribly peculiar Nazism presents itself as an example of degeneration in the German character. But one asks further, how could this take place — this astonishing deviation from the main lines of a European development which was apparently moving toward some kind of free-individualistic and binding-collectivist elements making toward the preservation of the liberal gains of the nineteenth century? Instead of a liberal tendency there came the precipitate shift to despotism, the rise of the *terribles simplificateurs* whom Jakob Burckhardt more than half a century ago saw coming. Burckhardt, more clearsighted than any other thinker of his time, also gives the first answers to our problem, which he understood at its first appearance. In the optimistic illusions of the Age of Enlightenment and the French Revolution he already perceived the germ of the great disease — the mistaken striving after the unattainable happiness of the masses of mankind, which then shifted into a desire for profits, power, and a general striving for living well. So there came about, Burckhardt further observes, the loosening of old social ties and ultimately the creation of new but very powerful ties by those men of violence, those *terribles simplificateurs,* who, supported by military organizations, forced the masses back again into discipline and obedience and a renunciation of all their former longings for freedom. In the misery of their daily existence they could then be called to position every morning by the beat of the drum and in the evening be led home again by the beat of the drum.

It was thus as a Western, and not merely as a German, problem — as the historical problem of a declining culture in general — that Burckhardt saw these things taking place. The example of France, the shift there twice from democracy to Caesarism, bemused his historical and prophetic phantasy. His conception remains a grand one in any case, even though one may reproach him with a certain overemphasis arising from his moralizing. The whole process looks like the moral degeneration of European society — of the masses as well as of the leading classes. And yet there were irresistible, dynamic forces also at work. The simultaneous industrial revolution was just as successful as the French Revolution with its mobilization of the masses, and the awakening of an urge to freedom, power and profits. Beginning first in England in the economic and technical field as a result of machines, the industrial revolution gave rise to big business, new masses of population, and modern capitalism. The enormous pressure which the masses of the people, now multiplying much faster than ever before, exerted henceforth on the whole existing social order and civilization can hardly be overestimated. It arose not merely, as Burckhardt seems to suggest, from greed, but also from the elementary necessity of caring for the sorely neglected and amorphous new masses as worthy of human dignity.

The old society and the new masses — such henceforth was the framework within which everything developed in the nineteenth century, directly or indirectly, in the open or under cover, at the center or on the periphery. The masses pressed naturally at first toward democracy, and then beyond that, in order to safeguard fully their standard of living, to socialism. This became an ideology, a gospel for them; and a hoped-for revolution, which would upset everything and establish something new, was thought of as the means for attaining the millennial kingdom of human happiness. This danger, threatening from the side of the masses, surged up as a mighty wave which from the middle of the nineteenth century swept over the traditional culture of the world. A mastery over it, however, was soon secured, partly through preventive, repressive, or reforming domestic measures, partly and much more by the fact that a second mighty wave had already risen up out of the expanding life of the masses and the nations. This second wave flooded crosswise over the first, more or less weakening or diverting it; its aim was not a fundamental social revolution but the increase of the political power of the nation. This second wave was none other than the nationalist movement of the nineteenth century, which originally was also a liberal movement aiming at the individual's rights to freedom. But after the rights to freedom had been won and seemed secured, nationalism and the desire for political power came more and more into the foreground as motivating forces. In its beginnings the national wave was by no means in harmony with the traditional state system: here and there it thrust against it with revolutionary force. It differed, however, from the other socialistic wave in not being so fundamentally hostile to the old European world, and, even in time, in being able to enter into alliance with it. It gathered its main body of adherents not from the new industrial proletarian masses who had been left amorphous and who were becoming desperate, but from the educated middle class which was enriching itself. This middle class, in its breadth, its growing well-being, and its self-consciousness, was a result of the transformations described above which took place in the old European society after the end of the eighteenth century. The component elements of this middle class were indeed old, as old as town life itself. But its expansion and integral growth in the great wave of the nationalist movement was made possible only through the rapid increase of the masses of the population since the beginning of the nineteenth century. This population increase was the most elemental as well as the dynamically strongest cause of the process of transformation taking place throughout the West.

In saying this we are not disloyal to the idea that spiritual factors are of primary importance in history. We distinguish between causalities and values in history, and we are now trying to understand fully the force of the crudest and most elemental causality which in this case is the pressure of the new masses on the old society. We are taking the trouble to understand it only because in the final analysis upon it depends the fate of the spiritual values of the West. For now that these values are mortally threatened by the consequences of the catastrophe we have suffered, we are doubly bound to understand the dark, elemental foundation of all that is glorious and holy in our Western, especially in our German national culture. By "causes," which form a connection between causalities and values, we mean not merely the purely mechanical but also the deep and hidden relations of life.

We spoke of the relation in which the two great waves of the nineteenth century, the socialist and the national movements, stood to one another. The imminent final revolution, the great smash or *Kladderadatsch* prophesied by the leaders of the socialist movement did not take place at once, because the national factor was more vocal and was able to extend itself. It grew into nationalism, and in the case of the great powers into imperialism, and so by the end of the nineteenth century rose sharply. People worried about the war of competition between the national economies for living space for the coming generations. Increases of power through the building up of army and navy and through colonial as well as commercial expansion overseas became the order of the day. *Post equitem sedet atra cura,* wrote a highly gifted young economist, Paul Voigt, in the *Preussische Jahrbücher* in 1898. In quoting this, he was thinking of industrial exports, as he feverishly examined the world markets. At the same time he painted in detail the possibility of an English blockade of Germany, which would result in suffering like that during the Thirty Years' War and also in Russian domination over

Germany. After the opening of the twentieth century, the question of who should have the widest place in the sun was drifting toward a settlement by war. The leaders of the socialist movement exhausted themselves in declamations against this drift, but they could do nothing to check it. Not socialism but imperialism was the order of the day in world history when World War I broke out.

Great revulsion of feeling followed the war. Russian as well as German imperialism was frustrated in its attempt to overshadow socialism, and to use its million-men armies (a typical fruit of the mighty population increase) to carry out the aims of the nationalistic bourgeoisie. The socialist wave now mounted mightily again, above all in Russia where it rose into Bolshevik Communism. In Germany, on the other hand, the socialism which came to power in 1918 took a more lower-middle-class direction, emphasized therefore more the democratic part of its program, and renounced all the imperialist aims of the nationalistic bourgeoisie. In the victor states of Western Europe and North America, after all their military successes, no clear decision was reached between the imperialist idea and the socialist idea but in general the upper middle class maintained its position.

Could the two great waves of the West remain in the long run separated from one another? Could there be anything but struggle and opposition between them? Or could some inner intermingling of them be successful? Such an intermingling, if it was attempted and failed, could indeed bring a frightful calamity upon the country and upon the whole world — as happened, in fact, in World War II. One must admit, however, that each of the two waves, the nationalist and the socialist, could claim for itself a deep historical justification. They were by no means, as Burckhardt's ideas might imply, merely the offspring of this or that form of human greed. They were, on the contrary, instinctive groping efforts to solve the human problems resulting from a population increase everywhere unprecedented in the history of the world. We recognized, for instance, even in imperialism — the

mischief-maker for world peace — the anxiety for the economic means of existence for a country's own people. And a
very similar anxiety was alive in socialism, though it sought
a wholly different path for its alleviation. Let us postpone
until later the answer to the question whether, and if so, how,
the claim of one wave could be brought into harmony with
that of the other, and fix our attention now on the attempts
actually made to intermingle both waves. We shall confine
ourselves to the experiments made in Italy and in Germany.

With this intermingling of the nationalist and socialist
waves there was united in these experiments the idea of giving hardness and firmness to the combination by means of an
authoritarian, centralized control over state, nation, and individuals, free from all checks of a parliamentary nature. A
whole world of ideals, hitherto faithfully revered, was eclipsed
by this authoritarian control — ideals not only liberal and
humanitarian directed toward the individual's freedom and
happiness, but also old Christian ideals in so far as they aimed
at the welfare of the individual soul. Christianity through its
concern for the individual soul is indeed the mother-earth of
liberalism, which in turn can be regarded as secularized
Christianity.

In the new authoritarian systems of Italy and Germany,
however, it was not the individual human being who was all
important but the totality of the individual souls firmly
welded together. The individual soul lost its identity and
worth in the totality. It was a monstrous revolution, an im-
measurable loss of existing cultural values that would have
been bearable only if the new way of life had been able to
create new and undreamed-of cultural values. And did the
totality gain everything that it wanted to gain by sucking into
itself all the sap and strength of the individual souls?

Italy, for our purpose here, requires only a few words. The
strait-jacket of Fascism was thoroughly unsuited to the Italian
national character. The Italian people, rich in creative talents
and imperishable contributions to civilization, are not at all
a soldier people. They were not adequate to the task put upon
them by Mussolini of raising Italy to the rank of a world

power. The only thing about Fascism that was really congenial to the Italians was Mussolini's rhetorical skill, his ability to intoxicate himself with air-castles of glory and grandeur. By understanding how to rattle his sword without ever having actually to draw it in a really great conflict, Mussolini succeeded for nearly two decades in maintaining himself and in evoking the semblance of a higher place for Italy among the great powers. The fact that in 1940, after Germany's undreamed-of great victory over France, he became Hitler's accomplice — perhaps forced to this in order not to lose his prestige and authority — led him down the road to his destruction. Without Hitler, if he had continued to follow his previous tactics, he might perhaps have been able to maintain himself for a long time.

Mussolini's efforts after 1940 suffered from another fundamental weakness: Italy was not sufficiently provided with raw materials and food to enter into competition with world powers. The same was true even of Germany, though she was somewhat better off in this respect than Italy. Experience has shown this, and any sober observer after the First World War could have said so. It was a rash venture for Germany to want to become a world power. The utter rashness, however, of her undertaking became clear only during the Second World War, which Hitler and his party conjured up. What roots in the history of the German people did this venture have? The following chapters will attempt to give the answer.

2 THE GERMAN PEOPLE BEFORE AND AFTER
THE FOUNDING OF THE EMPIRE

One can best start with the fact that the two great waves of the nineteenth century, the national and the socialist movements, had a wholly peculiar character in Germany and at the same time reacted upon one another. They perhaps crisscrossed and fought each other more sharply than in other countries and thereby developed fighting qualities which, when the historic moment arrived for their intermingling, were to be fatal because of the manner in which the intermingling was finally attempted. This general formula will now be explained by setting forth the particulars.

In Germany the national wave set in decidedly earlier, about half a century earlier, than the socialist wave. A new bourgeois middle class appeared on the scene much earlier than the new proletarian masses. The economic-technical revolution, the basic cause of the growth of the proletariat, began to set in later than in Western Europe. The fact that the bourgeois class, on the other hand, grew strong earlier and came to a rich intellectual flowering was surely enhanced by an improvement in its condition which had already taken place in the eighteenth century.

A national movement in the full sense of the word, in which there is a national feeling not only in individuals and small groups but also in whole classes of the people, can be said to have existed only after the foreign Napoleonic domination and the War of Liberation. With the national movement certain changes in the character of the German people began to take place — changes which one must know in order in some way to understand Germany's destiny. About 1815 and later Wilhelm von Humboldt, with his eminent fineness of feeling, observed a change which from his standpoint betokened both a gain and a loss — possibly more loss than gain. He looked upon the patriotically inspired warriors of the war and believed that a new, greater, nobler character had developed in them, but one which was more tied to reality than was his or Goethe's generation, which had been able to live on a plane above reality.

This stronger grasp of reality now increased from decade to decade; there was a relaxation of the desire for the transcendental, higher, and eternal way of living. Now, as Goethe said, men desired only wealth and speed. The new magic inventions of the steam-engine and railroad begat the new cult of coal and iron. The new realism also took possession of spiritual life. It put an end to the way of living aimed solely at the advancement and enrichment of one's own individuality. It directed attention more to corporate living in masses, to the structure of society, and to the nation as a whole. In addition, there were the well-known motive forces of a political sort: the opposition to the police state and the desire for written constitutions in order to help the middle class to power. So the way was prepared for the Revolution of 1848, which was not merely a cry for greater freedom but, as Dahlmann once said, in larger part a cry for power.

The modern man of power in Germany, however, as we have ultimately experienced him with terror, was still far from completed. There were still several intermediate stages between the Goethe period and the Bismarck period and between the Bismarck period and the Hitler period. And at each new stage one could perhaps detect, if he listened carefully, the pushing of the masses of the population who were becoming ever more numerous and demanding. The masses were advancing, as Hegel is believed to have already said, and their quantitative increase translated itself into qualitative differences.

About the middle of the nineteenth century and later it was the high aim of German culture to preserve from this pressure and from its coarsening and deteriorating effect the sacred heritage of the Goethe period — an almost miraculous gift bestowed upon the German people — and at the same time to support strongly what seemed vital and fruitful in the demands of the new masses. There was to be a synthesis of intellect and force, of the intellect-building and the state-building factors, and therewith of culture, state and nation. In this synthesis, however, there was a slight preponderance on the side of the new ideas of power and nationalism. Such was the painstaking purpose of a group of intellectual leaders in Germany who are customarily known as the "classical liberals" and who at the end of the fifties found their organ in the *Preussische Jahrbücher*. Heinrich von Treitschke was perhaps their greatest, at any rate their most influential, representative. An abundance of notable heads showed up there, a rich and wonderful group, if we consider their lives and the deeper content of their writings. Compared with Goethe's era, to be sure, it was only a silver as contrasted with a golden age, because somewhat inferior successors gave the tint to it. Compared with the cultural level of today, however, it was overtopping. This attempt at one and the same time to recognize strongly opposed forces and yet let them fructify each other was a special German phenomenon that has no analogies either in Russia or in France and England, though possibly in Italy's Risorgimento movement. It wanted to soar to the skies and yet keep a firm foot on earth, to bring the rights of free and proud individuality into harmonious accord with the collectivist powers of the state and nation. But was this in the long run generally possible? Was it possible under the concrete conditions existing in Germany?

The synthesis which the classical liberals tried to bring about was seriously threatened by two dangers, then gradually undermined in the course of decades, and finally destroyed. The first danger consisted of the two social groups that the synthesis tried directly to guide and force into union with one another. The groups were the Prussian state with its monarchical military structure and the upper middle class, part of which was more interested in making profits and part more interested in creative work. The second danger for the success of the synthesis sprang from the fundamental fact of the nineteenth century that has already been emphasized: the mutual crisscrossing of the two waves — the national movement based on the middle class and the socialist movement based on the growing masses.

In the Prussian state of Frederick William I and Frederick the Great there lived two souls, one capable of culture and the other hostile to culture. The Prussian army as created by Frederick William I brought forth a remarkably penetrating militarism that influenced all civil life and found its like in no neighboring state. However, as early as the travel sketches of Montesquieu, who lived in Hanoverian territory near the

Prussian frontier, we find some unpleasant things about it. The question of the origin of Prussian militarism we can leave to one side; we wish to inquire here only into its influence on German destiny as a whole in the nineteenth century.

As long as the synthesis of intellect and power seemed to look hopeful in the nineteenth century, we regarded even militarism with a more benevolent eye; we emphasized the undoubtedly high moral qualities which were evident in it: the iron sense of duty, the ascetic strictness in service, the disciplining of the character in general. Easily overlooked, however, was the fact that this disciplining developed a leveling habit of conformity of mind which narrowed the vision and also often led to a thoughtless subserviency toward all higher authorities. This habit of conformity caused many of the richer springs of life to dry up. Furthermore, the advocates of Prussian militarism overlooked at first the fact that all sorts of unlovely practices and passions could rage under cover of exterior discipline. Public life also might suffer from these effects of militarism if the statesmen and generals, who had grown comfortably important in the militarist atmosphere, had an influence on the life of the nation. This evil seemed apparent even at the time of the War of Liberation, when the synthesis of intellect and state was for the first time boldly attempted. The synthesis was in many ways brilliantly attested, but ultimately was fatally crippled by a militarily narrow-minded monarch and by an equally narrow-minded and at the same time egotistical caste of nobles and officers. The crippling of the reform movement, symbolized in 1819 by the dismissal of Wilhelm von Humboldt and Boyen, may be regarded as a victory in the Prussian state of the soul that was hostile to culture over the soul that was capable of culture. The rift ran straight through the whole nineteenth century and was inherited by the twentieth century. Finally, Prussian militarism also secured a large place for itself in the mixing pot into which Adolf Hitler threw together all substances and essences of German development which he found usable.

However, in the era when the Empire was founded, the aspects of Prussian militarism which were bad and dangerous for the general well-being were obscured by the imposing proof of its power and discipline in its service for national unity and in the construction of Bismarck's Empire. The military man now seemed to be a consecrated spirit — the lieutenant moved through the world as a young god and the civilian reserve lieutenant at least as a demigod. He had to rise to be reserve officer in order to exert his full influence in the upper-middle-class world and above all in the state administration. Thus militarism penetrated civilian life. Thus there developed a conventional Prussianism (*Borussismus*), a naïve self-admiration in Prussian character, and together with it a serious narrowing of intellectual and political outlook. Everything was dissolved into a rigid conventionalism. One must have observed this type in countless examples with one's own eyes in the course of a long life, one must have felt it in one's own self, struggled with it, and gradually liberated one's self from it, in order to understand its power over men's minds — in order to understand finally the effect of the touching comedy in the Potsdam church on March 21, 1933, which Hitler played with Hindenburg beside the tomb of Frederick the Great. For here National Socialism was expected to appear as the heir and propagator of all the great and beautiful Prussian traditions.

A man like Theodore Fontane, whose lifework represents as none other all that was great and beautiful in the Prussian tradition, could, in a letter written in 1897, near the end of his life when he had grown critical and keen of insight, utter words of displeasure about the Prussian world around him. His testimony is not to be rejected simply because it is sharply exaggerated in every direction. "Borussism," he wrote, "is the lowest form of culture that has ever existed. Only Puritanism is still worse, because it is completely given to lying." And another time he wrote: "What must be crushed first of all is militarism."

This evil Borussism and militarism was like a heavy mortgage imposed on Bismarck's work and inherited from him by his hybrid successor, Hitler. There was, however, also something in the immediate contribution of Bismarck himself which lay on the border between good and evil and which in its further development was to expand more on the side of evil. The truth of this criticism would never be readily conceded by those who grew great under Bismarck's work and richly enjoyed its blessings. We Germans often felt so free and proud, in contrast with the whole previous German past, in this mightily flourishing Empire of 1871 which gave living space to every one of us! But the staggering course of World War I and still more of World War II makes it impossible to pass over in silence the query whether the germs of the later evil were not really implanted in Bismarck's work from the outset. It is a query which courageous and unfettered historical thinking must pose in regard to every great and apparently beneficent historical phenomenon in which a degeneration takes place. One then breathes the atmosphere of the tragedy of history, of human and historical greatness, and also the problematical uncertainty which will ever hover around a Bismarck and his work — while Hitler's work must be reckoned as the eruption of the satanic principle in world history.

Consider now the year 1866 and Bismarck's blood and iron policy. Today we listen with more emotion to the voices which at that time expressed concern over the great evils of the future — voices of such important men as Jakob Burckhardt and Constantin Frantz, and one might add as a third the queer Swabian, Christian Planck. Bismarck's policy, according to them, was destroying certain foundations of Western culture and the community of states and was a really deep-reaching revolution which was opening the prospect of further revolutions and an era of wars. It meant, they said, the victory of Machiavellism over the principles of morality and justice in international relations and it let perish the finer and higher things of culture in a striving after power and pleasure.

Let us be honest. However one-sided these complaints may have been, there is a grain of truth in them. On the other hand, there are plenty of voices to defend Bismarck. They call attention to all the similar examples of Machiavellian practices in the rest of Europe of that day and especially to the fact that Bismarck himself recognized limits to his policy of force. These defenders likewise point out that in his peace policy after 1871 Bismarck did good service to the Western community of nations. "You know I cannot love Bismarck," a Danish historian friend said to me during the Third Reich, "but now I must say: Bismarck belongs to *our* world."

One must regard Bismarck as a borderline case. He still had in mind to some extent the conception of a synthesis of power and culture as it was understood by the leaders of the movement for German unity. These leaders themselves, with Treitschke at their head, originally were seriously offended by Bismarck's first steps in the period of the constitutional conflict, but became his defenders and admirers as a consequence of the war of 1866. The result was that in the synthesis of power and culture, of the things of the state and the things of the spirit, the preponderance slowly but steadily shifted further over to the side of power and its domain. From my own development I can bear witness to this — until, in the years before the First World War, a reaction of humanitarian feeling once more began to set in.

One can always object that the power-state and Machiavellism were not confined to Germany, that they were more often preached but not more strongly practiced by us Germans. This view is quite true. Specifically German, however, was the frankness and nakedness of the German power-state and Machiavellism, its hard and deliberate formulation as a principle of conduct, and the pleasure taken in its reckless consequences. Specifically German also was the tendency to elevate something primarily practical into a universal world-view theory. It was a serious thing for the future that these ideas about power-state and Machiavellism, at first expressed merely as theories, might become practical weapons in the hands of ruling authorities. The German power-state idea, whose history began with Hegel, was to find in Hitler its worst and most fatal application and extension.

The degeneration of the German people is what we are here trying, by groping and probing, to understand merely in its rough outlines. How difficult it is, however, to sketch a picture of the spiritual and cultural condition of Germany in the first decades after the founding of the Empire in 1871, of the good as well as the bad germs in it! The judgment commonly expressed today, often merely parroting Nietzsche, that liberalism had become flat and shallow, settles nothing. The silver age of classical liberalism, of which we spoke, still persisted and still produced in art and science much that was brilliant, while the average level and everyday taste remained decidedly low. But no one then would have thought possible the emergence in educated Germany of a phenomenon like National Socialism — only the uneducated, proletarian Germany of Social Democracy was feared as a serious menace to our culture in the future. We, especially we younger Germans, felt exceedingly safe, entirely too safe, in the possession of a high national and cultural heritage. Here and there, however, clouds began to appear in this bright sky.

The anti-Semitic movement at the beginning of the eighties brought the first flash of lightning. The Jews, who were inclined to enjoy indiscreetly the favorable economic situation now smiling upon them, had since their full emancipation aroused resentment of various sorts. They contributed much to that gradual depreciation and discrediting of the liberal world of ideas that set in after the end of the nineteenth century. The fact that besides their negative and disintegrating influence they also achieved a great deal that was positive in the cultural and economic life of Germany was forgotten by the mass of those who now attacked the damage done by the Jewish character. Out of the anti-Semitic feeling it was possible for an anti-liberal and an anti-humanitarian feeling to develop easily — the first steps toward National Socialism. In the popularity which the anti-Semitic rector Ahlwardt, a man of the crudest half-education, enjoyed in the early eighties, one can see the soft prelude to Hitler's later success. But people would have laughed if any one at that time had predicted to us such a success. We Germans felt all too secure in our firmly established state based on the reign of law, in our comfortable civil order, in our liberal ideals — still ever shining in spite of their paling — of freedom, self-determination, and human dignity.

The whole bourgeois world, whether anti-Semitic or pro-Semitic, was still borne along on one of the two waves which swept through the nineteenth century — the wave of the national movement. But this was crisscrossed, as has already been said, by the second great wave — the socialist movement which arose from the masses of the industrial proletariat. We shall limit ourselves here to the attempt to explain what this second movement, by its inherent tendencies as well as by its reaction upon the bourgeois world, may have meant for the rise of National Socialism.

The socialist state that was the goal of the future could be realized only as a state which was to a high degree authoritarian and which organized daily life thoroughly. It remained at first a dream of the future and the thinking of the masses was certainly more concerned with the needs, cares, and desires of daily life than with it. One may suspect, however, that it helped materially to collectivize the masses and to modify deeply their feeling about legal rights; that is, the rights of the individual grew dimmer and the rights of the total state over the individual were allowed to become continually stronger. The phrase "prison state" was flung in reproach at the socialists because that described, so it was said, what they were trying to set up. On the other hand, the anger and hate of those who felt exploited toward the other traditional social groups, who were regarded as reactionary, directly undermined the feeling for traditional historical authority in general. Hatred inflamed the revolutionary recklessness with which people trampled upon the rights and property of their opponents. So there developed a revolutionary spirit in general, to which National Socialism could later fall heir. The thing that was astonishing and characteristic of German development was the fact that this revolutionary spirit could change its bearers and could somehow leap from the class of the industrial proletariat, which had carried it hitherto, to other social classes now arising, some for the first time. We shall speak later of this process.

Within the Social Democratic range of ideas, however, alongside of the long-prevailing revolutionary solution of the problem of the future, there was also another *evolutionary* solution. It counted on a gradual, step-by-step amelioration and transformation of the social situation and on successes, small at first but cumulative, in the struggle of the workers against the capitalist world. The goal of a completely new reordering of the social world was not thereby abandoned, but was pushed off into the distant future.

Such "revisionist" ideas, to be sure, could begin to prevail over orthodox revolutionary Marxism only after actual developments toward the turn of the century had become favorable to them. Not increasing misery, as the revolutionary theory demanded, but a perceptible improvement of the standard of living of the German working classes took place. And no longer was there *one* mass of all the other classes interested in capitalism standing in hostile opposition to them. The formerly integrated opposition was loosened as it was caught in the stream of development: a part was quite willing to make concessions to the workers and another part was quite hardened in its determination to fight any threatening revolution with the most determined reaction. The evolutionists in one camp found justification and support in the evolutionists of the other camp, and the rank revolutionists found an echo and to a certain extent a historical counterpart in the rank reactionaries. Such was the general course of the interaction of the two great waves of the bourgeois national movement and of the proletarian socialist movement. Let us make this clear in detail.

The evolutionary side of the story rests on two basic facts, one purely economic, the other resulting from a combination of political, social, and moral factors. The purely economic fact was the tremendous economic upsurge since the nineties, which brought well-being and wealth to the bourgeoisie, and also gradually brought better wage opportunities and a slow rise in the standard of living to the workers. Even before this upsurge, an idea of social reform existed in the state and among the bourgeoisie. It took practical shape in the social security insurance legislation during the eighties toward the close of the Bismarck era. Among the bourgeoisie there was an agitation in various quarters to carry this social reform further and make it even more effective. In the nineties Friedrich Naumann took the most radical lead in this matter through his national socialist movement which had as its organ the magazine *Hilfe* (Help).

Let us look at the deeper historical significance of this movement. It demanded for the future the merging together in a powerful union of the two great waves, the bourgeois-national and the proletarian-socialist. Such a union was, as we said at the outset, highly desirable and even vital for the entire nation because in both waves a deep and justifiable ferment which could be historically fruitful was at work. For these waves to continue ever crisscrossing and interfering with each other could not remain the last word in their history. In each of the waves, however, there was also a tendency to mount too high, to be dangerously one-sided. If the union was to be successful, there had to be moderation in each of the movements; they had to be united somehow at the point where what was harmful in each did not get the upper hand.

Now Naumann's attempt, though it was greeted with great enthusiasm by the German bourgeois and idealistically inclined youth, did not succeed, as is well known, in bringing about a union of the two waves — that is, in bringing the bourgeoisie and the working classes into harmony in regard to the great basic questions of public life. Had Naumann been successful, there probably would never have been a Hitler movement.

Naumann's national socialism, looked at from a purely rational and cultural point of view, was a wonderful attempt to bring together in an exceedingly rich synthesis both the most spiritual and the most practical and realistic elements in the German people. Christianity and German idealism, the classical ideal of humanity and modern social empiricism, democracy and empire, the modern feeling of the need for art, for a people's system of national defense, for economic expansion — all these ideas were now to stand like good fairies beside the cradle of the New Germany and present it with a birthday present. Even from the feared fairy of Marxism certain truths which it represented were to be received. The synthesis of classical liberalism was perpetuated, but was developed further into what was practical and suited to the soil. So the substantial requirements of the masses as well as the finer requirements of the cultural classes were to be satisfied; also the need for culture among the masses was to be recognized and as far as possible satisfied.

It was one of the noblest dreams in German hisory, but a dream which came at a time, partly too early and partly too late, to be actually realized. However, the little which it did accomplish ought not to be unduly undervalued. One can see that before the First World War the Naumann movement, even after it had failed as an independent political party, helped to create bridges and possibilities of understanding between the bourgeoisie and the working classes. It encouraged and spiritually enriched the revisionist movement within Social Democracy. In the exaltation and feeling of brotherhood during the August days of 1914 there lay something of the ethos and pathos of Naumann's dream.

In order to see this connection in full light, we must now go a little beyond the time limits of this chapter. Whether one estimates the Naumann influence on the revisionist development as greater or less, the fact is nevertheless that an important part of the total development, namely, the path which the majority of the Social Democratic working classes henceforth followed, corresponded exactly with Naumann's wishes and hopes. From the outset of the World War the working classes no longer stood in deadly hostility toward the bourgeois world. They were ready to coöperate with it, and no fair-minded thinker could gainsay their patriotic national feeling. The workingmen were therefore ripening toward the solution of the great historical task of uniting the two waves of the era, the national and the socialist movements. They penetrated henceforth the petty bourgeoisie by their pattern of life and practice. Among the best working-class elements there arose a spiritual longing to become participants in the treasures of German culture. Among the broad masses there prevailed a temperate materialism of a practical sort — while the doctrines of theoretical materialism and of Marxism, under whose influence the working-class movement had long stood, gradually grew dimmer. Among a minority of the working class, to be sure, the Marxian dogma remained intact, as the First World War showed, together with the revolutionary determination to overthrow the existing capitalist society. Whether this revolutionary determination of the German communists, supported by bolshevist Russia, would ever triumph would depend upon the world situation as a whole.

The world political situation, however, was not determined exclusively by the forces which played over us and independently of us. The shaping of these forces also always depended on what the German nation was willing and able to do. And the question of the causes of Germany's world political defeats and catastrophes must now lead us to another question: what were the wishes and abilities of the circles who led us and who influenced German world policy? What was their intellectual make-up and mentality? An examination will not lead to any such favorable conclusion as we can reach for the working class as a whole. The co-responsibility and blame of the German bourgeoisie for everything which prepared the way for the catastrophes, and especially for the rise of National Socialism, is not small.

We have already dealt with the beginnings of this sinister development in the German bourgeoisie and shown how the synthesis of classical liberalism shifted to the disadvantage of the cultural features, how national egoism and the state-power idea more and more repressed the cosmopolitan and humane elements. Even a man like Treitschke, when he was old, felt this to be a serious loss: it is apparent in the tone of his lectures on politics. Whoever today reads the *Preussische Jahrbücher* of these decades can follow clearly the course of this story. Its editor, Hans Delbrück, was one of the earliest of those who recognized the shifting of forces and saw most clearly the dangers to German policy springing from it. He wrote in 1899 (volume 95):

It was the high ideal of our fathers that the German national state should come into existence without the Germans deteriorating into the hatefulness and exclusiveness which in the case of other countries we brand as Chauvinism, Jingoism, Moscowism. The firm authority of the state was to go hand in hand with the free unfolding of individuality which for no people is more indispensable, because no people are more richly endowed with it than our own. The nobler minds are beginning to see with horror the forms which the national feeling is now taking and the kinds of men who are presuming to take over the leadership in national questions. The state authority manifests itself as excessive officiousness and police arbitrariness. The management that naturally belongs to propertied people is degenerating into class rule, and all these evil forces are combining to imprison the free German spirit behind the bars which they prescribe for it. All this is only in its beginnings, but the beginnings are here. One must take care that a stop is put to them before it is too late.

Delbrück's words sum up with sharp insight the observations that he had to make during this period to certain circles of the propertied bourgeoisie and to the still powerful nobility in the state service. Within the foreign and domestic arena and in many places there were various conflicting groups. Within them there was the same narrow spirit threatening total damage to the state, to culture, and to the people — a danger later to occur, but in a stormier way, in the beginnings of National Socialism. The free, humane culture which came down from the days of Goethe was threatened by the narrowing and hardening of the national idea.

Also threatened by this hardening process was the task of setting Germany's goals in world politics which at the turn of the century entered upon a decisive stage. We have already shown at the outset how hot and dangerous for Germany was the ground of world policy which she now had to tread for the preservation of her vital economic interests in the future. We heard Paul Voigt's warning about the effects of an extended English blockade on Germany's whole future. Only a very carefully considered, very cautious and moderate world policy was possible in this precarious situation. We Germans were still only in the first stages of the crisis. The Pan-German movement with its overweening ambitions for conquest was highly dangerous, though not for the moment. It did us irreparable damage in the eyes of foreigners. It was also able gradually to pervert the mentality of our own bourgeoisie. Delbrück was henceforth tireless in combating it but with limited success.

In domestic politics the severe attitude of the master and employer opposed all suggestions and possibilities which sought to reform in a free and humane spirit the existing enforced relations among employees, employers and the state, as well as among the Poles in East Prussia, the Danes in North Schleswig, and the state. The Hakatists in Posen and West Prussia, the blusterers in big business, and the Junker bureaucrats in the ministries and the provincial governments were all concrete agents in this domestic state power system that was now the complement of the Pan-German movement in foreign affairs.

However strongly one may emphasize the differences between the unsocial "master" psychology of those times and of Hitler's National Socialism, it was, if looked at as part of the whole development, a step toward National Socialism.

There existed at the turn of the century a great deal of good old bourgeois culture which as a matter of course, in spite of the increasing superficiality of life, put certain moral restraints on political ambitions. Friedrich Naumann's national socialist movement more or less aimed at the very opposite of what the threatening coalition of blusterers, Hakatists, and Pan-Germans aimed at. The two streams in the bourgeois camp met most closely in the field of world politics, in the demand for armed participation in the struggles for the partition of the world and for securing Germany's living space in the future. All the bourgeois elements merged together in the movement for building the navy, as to whose size, to be sure, people had no clear conception. In case of serious danger this merger of interests would have held together just as little as it held together during the First World War. Fundamentally the bad and the good mentors of the German bourgeoisie at this time were completely divorced.

Germany was not the only country into which the evil penetrated. One must say today that the whole imperialist movement of the Western nations was responsible for creating the conditions for the impending political as well as cultural disaster of the West, even though one may also recognize the inevitability of imperialism and its solicitude for the future of one's own people. Every requirement of this kind, however, bears within itself new germs of evil, and the extent of the evil depends essentially upon the measure of insight and caution in the intellectual and moral make-up of the leading circles among the people. No people had more reason to exercise caution and moderation than the Germans in their shut-in and endangered position and with their tendency to exaggerate ideas which they have once seized upon. We may quote here the words of a noble philosopher, Friedrich Paulsen, in 1902, also from the *Preussische Jahrbücher* (volume 110, page 173); they express the growing alarm of humane-minded patriots:

A supersensitive nationalism has become a very serious danger for all the peoples of Europe; because of it, they are in danger of losing the feeling for human values. Nationalism, pushed to an extreme, just like sectarianism, destroys moral and even logical consciousness. Just and unjust, good and bad, true and false, lose their meaning; what men condemn as disgraceful and inhuman when done by others, they recommend in the same breath to their own people as something to be done to a foreign country.

There you have the ethics of Hitler's National Socialism.

We have reached here only the first stages of the process of degeneration in the German bourgeoisie. The two decades prior to the outbreak of the First World War were an era of the strongest counterforces vying with one another and an era of uncertain possibilities for the future. Out of the same bourgeoisie came both the hardening nationalism of the Pan-Germans and the national socialist movement of Friedrich Naumann. And however unconditionally the drive for wealth and power seemed to proceed in the managerial circles of this bourgeoisie, these two decades before the First World War were nevertheless filled at the same time with a new idealistic striving, with a renewing of ties with the Goethe golden age, ties which were by no means merely imitative but were also creative. A quite special, modern spirit arose, particularly in art and poetry. Truth, sincerity, and inwardness can be seen as the guiding stars of these new tendencies, often combined with a radical determination to break down on the way all restraints imposed by the previously existing world. At the same time, to be sure, there were the fatal threads of connection with the rising amoral nationalism with which we have become acquainted as the immediate prelude to Hitlerism. In Nietzsche's realm of ideas, which now began to exert a powerful influence over all yearning and restless spirits, there were gathered together almost all the noble and ignoble desires and self-longings which filled this period — a demonic phenomenon in the disruptiveness of its character and influence. It was predominantly harmful. Nietzsche's superman, destroying the old tables of morality, guided like a mysteriously seductive beacon an unfortunately not small part of the German youth, guided it forward into a wholly dark future which must be conquered.

3 THE GERMAN PEOPLE DURING THE FIRST WORLD WAR

When the First World War broke out, it seemed once more that a kind angel might lead the German people back to the right path. The exaltation of spirit experienced during the August days of 1914, in spite of its ephemeral character, is one of the most precious, unforgettable memories of the highest sort. All the rifts which had hitherto existed in the German people, both within the bourgeoisie and between the bourgeoisie and the working classes, were suddenly closed in the face of the common danger which snatched us out of the security of the material prosperity that we had been enjoying. And more than that, one perceived in all camps that it was not a matter merely of the unity of a gain-seeking partnership, but that an inner renovation of our whole state and culture was needed. We generally believed indeed that this had already commenced and that it would progress further in the common experiences of the war, which was looked upon as a war of defense and self-protection. We underwent a rare disappointment in our hopes. Within a year the unity was shattered and the German people were again separated upon various paths. Was the uplift of August 1914 after all merely the last flickering of older evolutionary forces which were now coming to an end? A good observer, Max Hildebert Böhm, suspected as much in 1917. He wrote in the *Preussische Jahrbücher* (volume 167): "In many respects August 1914 will perhaps at a later time look much less like the commencement of a new era than the rather painful farewell to an old one, the splendid final harmonious note of a romanticism from which the German mind could tear itself away only with profound resignation." The new era that is now really approaching, he continued, will be characterized by techniques, rationalism, bread-rationing socialism, by a pitiless ethos guided not by the heart but by the head. "A state whose essence is organization will be indifferent, with the innermost distrust, toward the incalculable unfolding of life of the individual, from which alone German culture buds forth."

These words like a searchlight throw their beam both backward and forward. We stand at the main turning-point in the evolution of the German people. The man of Goethe's day was a man of free individuality. He was at the same time a "humane" man, who recognized his duty toward the community to be "noble, helpful, and good" and carried out his duty accordingly. He lived and developed at first in the synthesis of classical liberalism and then of the national socialism of the Naumann stamp. He became ever more strongly bound up with the social needs of the masses and with the political requirements of the state; that is, he became ever more tightly and concretely united with the community of people and state that enveloped him. Once more something of this old free relationship between the individual and the state glowed in the romanticism of the August days. Was the "humane" man, who then once again bore testimony to himself, henceforth to be condemned to extinction by all the forces which were compressing men more and more in masses? We shall keep this difficult question in mind; the answer to it can be found, so far as is possible at all, at the end.

As early as 1915 one could perceive that the August synthesis of cultural and social forces would not last. It crumbled away simultaneously from both the right and the left. The efforts of the extreme left, associated with the name of the younger Liebknecht, belong to the history of communism in Germany. Communism was developing and would become of historical significance if Germans of the future should take their stamp from it. The developments on the German right wing which must now occupy us were not yet, however, touched by communism.

The conflict about war aims broke out at this point. For Germany's future the important thing to be done now was for Germany to extricate herself from the mortally dangerous position into which she had fallen through her thoughtless prewar policy. She had made enemies simultaneously of the two great world powers, Russia and England. To put through Germany's full demands in world politics in the face of this double enmity simply exceeded her physical capacity. If any gain at all was to be hoped for, it would have to be a modest one. Even a peace which merely preserved the existing situation for us Germans, like the Peace of Hubertusburg at the end of the Seven Years' War, should have been deemed a "victory." Only a few men, however, in the leading circles of the bourgeoisie could elevate themselves to this moderate view. They were the men in whom the synthesis of classical liberalism was still working and in whom the classical ideal of humanity and the feeling for the community of Western culture and for moderation in victory were still alive. But in the great mass of the propertied and supposedly educated bourgeoisie there now prevailed those impulses which we already saw at the turn of the century: reckless national egoism, thoughtlessness in the choice of political means, indifference to the requirements of Europe's vital existence — all this combined with an uncritical overestimate of German political strength. This combination of impulses pretended to be realism in politics, but was the opposite of realism. The bourgeoisie flattered themselves, however, that they represented with conquering force the realism of modern men.

So there arose out of the conflict about war aims a conflict among the people themselves. Only as such can it be fully understood. Adequate words to express fully the nature of the two kinds of Germans are lacking. To call one type men of power (*Machtmenschen*) and the other men of culture (*Kulturmenschen*) would be a very clumsy way out of the difficulty, for their common educational background caused the men of power to pride themselves on their solicitude for culture, and the men of culture to pride themselves on their solicitude for power. On either side only the ingredient amount of culture or power was different. But once people became aware of how profoundly they differed in regard to definite problems (Belgium, Poland, the Baltic Provinces) the paths they had chosen necessarily separated them more and more widely. Many "men of power," to be sure, would have later energetically repudiated being mentioned in the same breath with Adolf Hitler. Nevertheless it was the path now chosen by the men of power that led to the regions in which Hitler later pitched his camp.

The paths chosen by the men of culture led to the regions in which the workingmen of the Majority Social Democratic party had already settled. One could agree with them in their temperate estimate of the war situation and in their rejection of utopian war aims and dreams of power. The international principle in German socialist thought, hitherto regarded as hostile to the nationalist principle, changed over into a complement of the national idea when the Social Democrats entered the National Front after August 1914. Again, the ingredient amount of the two elements of cosmopolitanism and state nationalism could turn out to be very varied.

In the field of domestic politics also the paths of the Social Democratic workingmen joined those of the men of culture, if we may use this inadequate expression. The worker justly demanded full equality of legal rights now that he had shown in the fight for the Fatherland that his contribution was as valuable as that of any other citizen. The previously existing fear that this equality of rights would deliver the state over to manipulation by the masses would abate if the development within the masses was healthy, if it cut loose from the revolutionary utopia, and if it pursued the good cultural ideals of the bourgeoisie. Such was now the case. Already during the war years a promising effort was begun to bring into inner harmony the two kinds of German people, one springing from the nationalist bourgeoisie, and the other from the socialist working classes. Even the old religious conflicts gave way before this new possibility. In the People's League for Freedom and Fatherland which was founded in the autumn of 1917 the Social Democratic and Christian trade unions joined in a common front with the humane-minded bourgeoisie. It was an exact prelude to the later Weimar Coalition of Center, Majority Socialist, and Democratic parties — the much-scorned "Weimar System."

Today, to be sure, we know only from those who were active in the People's League something of its existence, while the counter-league, the Fatherland party, likewise founded in the autumn of 1917, was talked about by every one. In fact, it was the Fatherland party which exerted the stronger influence on political action; it was able to exert pressure in combination with the Supreme Military Command upon the weak Imperial Government in the last days of the Monarchy. The Pan-German spirit of conquest as well as the domination in domestic politics of heavy industry and of the East German big landowners created for themselves in the Fatherland party an agency which dazzlingly concealed their true tendencies.

Many bourgeois elements at this time joined the Fatherland party with lively enthusiasm, under the illusion that it represented the true national interests. Among those who joined were cultivated men of a high level of mentality. One must look somewhat closer at this type of mankind, because in it the weaknesses of its spiritual structure can be seen especially clearly. The men of this type were men who joyfully endorsed in theory all the syntheses of classical liberalism, and yet, at the decisive moment when these syntheses were threatened, allowed themselves to be enticed away upon the path of deceptive and imaginary power-interests. There were trained officials, pastors, and court magistrates in abundance in the country who quickly rallied to what they believed was the assembly ground of a new national spirit, and they gladly overlooked the robust egoism of those who were now leading them. How lacking in judgment and how bound by conventionality the pastors, for instance, were can be seen in Rittelmeyer's beautiful memoirs.

In truth, the Fatherland party again widened the rifts between the bourgeoisie and the working classes and between the old monarchy and the new masses — rifts that had seemingly been bridged over during the August days of 1914. And as to foreign policy, the war was conducted under the influence of the Fatherland party in a way which could not ameliorate but only aggravate its outcome. For so long as the spirit of the Fatherland party and of the Pan-Germans behind it dominated Germany, there could be no thought of any readiness to make peace with the enemy, who became overpowering when North America entered the war. As a result of this situation, Delbrück wrote in the *Preussische Jahrbücher* on August 18, 1918: "The world demands, and has a right to demand, that the German people give a guarantee that the Pan-German spirit, the spirit of overbearing power, of hostility to good manners, and of paganism, is not the German spirit." And on August 29: "Not until we have stamped out Pan-Germanism, its war aims and its blasphemous preaching . . . not until then can the hour strike for the peace negotiations."

Are not these the phrases which also apply, word for word, to our whole situation during the Second World War? Can one doubt any longer that the Pan-Germans and the Fatherland party are an exact prelude to Hitler's rise to power?

4 THE POSTWAR SITUATION

When the collapse took place in the autumn of 1918, when the High Command decided to lay down its arms and the mutinies at Kiel set in motion the November revolution, the elements that had joined together in the Fatherland party began to turn about in a characteristic fashion. They did not want to admit that they had previously been following, with their illusions about annexations of territory and their postponement of domestic reforms, false paths, that is, policies that really promoted instead of preventing revolution. They now alleged that the military failure was caused by the revolution, instead of vice versa. They thus reversed the true order of cause and effect. For the real fact was that the army, fighting heroically in a struggle becoming more and more hopeless, had to yield before an inescapable and ever-increasing superior armed force. The "stab-in-the-back" legend, however, which now appeared in the right-wing camp — and can be proven to have really existed prior to the November revolution — alleged that victory was snatched from Germany because of the revolutionary disruption on the home front, under pressure of which the army commanders then had to lay down their arms. It is true that some beginnings of this disruption are to be found prior to August 1918, but it was not until after the military situation had become hopeless that the disruption increased to the point which led to revolution. By no means the least of the other false allegations which the representatives of the stab-in-the-back legend leveled against the so-called defeatists, that is, the men of the People's League, was the allegation that the defeatists had weakened the German will to fight by their preaching of moderation and by their whole humane attitude.

The Fatherland party and the stab-in-the-back legend represent the fatal turning point in the evolution of the German bourgeoisie. The decisive factor was that a large and important part of this bourgeoisie closed its mind more and more against the democratic idea — against the idea which aimed to close the rift between the bourgeoisie and the working classes and between the nationalist and socialist movements by recognizing an equality of rights for both groups and by building up a democratic form of government based on the will of the majority. To the part of the bourgeoisie which clung to the Fatherland party, however, this democratic form of government created by the Weimar Constitution of 1919 appeared in the scornful light of the stab-in-the-back legend as the product of disloyalty to the nation, as an unheroic attitude of mind, and as the selfish exploitation of a defeat caused by the treachery of the masses in their lust for power. Henceforth an open and a secret war was carried on against the Weimar Constitution by those elements which had coalesced in the Fatherland party in 1917–18. "The Weimar Constitution was destroyed at the dinner club (*Stammtisch*)," a shrewd observer, Siegfried von Kardorff, once said to me.

The Constitution was destroyed, that is, by the administrative gentlemen officials who dined together at the club and brought the Constitution into contempt by their exaggerated condemnation of its terms in the light of the stab-in-the-back theory. A drop of strong political poison thereby seeped into all official life after the war. These attacks on the Weimar Constitution were a mischievous attempt to revive suffering Germany, not through force or a dictatorship, but by assertions quietly uttered and approved at social gatherings.

The Weimar Constitution, to be sure, did suffer from defects, even from a sound democratic viewpoint. It provided too little firm and continuous authority at the top of the governmental structure and too great instability and dependence upon the shifting ups and downs of political parties. Even in the parties of the Weimar Coalition there were many unpleasant occurrences, shortsighted greediness for power, and, not least in influence, the fact that the working men and other groups now active had so long been deprived of a share in the government and had so suddenly come into the enjoyment of power. Among those who drank too hastily and greedily of the cup of power which had come to them were many Jews. They appeared in the eyes of persons with anti-Semitic feeling to be the beneficiaries of the German defeat and revolution. Everyone else in Germany, aside from these beneficiaries, seemed irrevocably consigned to misery.

The hand of the victor powers still lay heavy on us Germans in these early twenties. It is sufficient to mention the Versailles Treaty and to recall all the mental and material consequences which resulted from it. All private existence was shattered by the paper money inflation which wiped out all incomes and savings. In the bad year of 1923, when the French invaded the Ruhr, the inflation knew no bounds. There were also the psychological effects and the stab-in-the-back legend. Would we not have been actually the victors in the World War, people grimly thought to themselves, and have achieved victory in the end except for the treason within our own ranks? Many thousands of dismissed officers of the war's giant army now wandered penniless in the streets; they compared their former respected position with the misery of their present struggle for their daily bread; they felt like heroes whose dignity had been trampled upon. From the volunteer military companies (*Freiwilligenkorps*) which had taken a decisive part in suppressing communist disturbances after the war, came a mass of secret associations which were dreaming of a new uprising in the not too distant future. The Kapp Putsch in the spring of 1920 was the first, though it quickly failed. But when in the autumn of 1922 Mussolini's nationalist revolution in Italy met with success and his Fascist troops could begin their march on Rome without King Victor Emmanuel's regular army standing in their way, there awakened again among us Germans the urge to do something of the same kind — with the help, of course, of the small army (*Reichswehr*) which the Versailles Treaty had left to us. "The Reichswehr is ringed about with a network of black [that is, illegal] military associations," a well-informed man said to me at the time. The leader of the Reichswehr, General von Seeckt, of course behaved correctly as an obedient instrument of the democratic republican government, but the old Prussian-German militarism, with its brilliant qualities as well as with the narrowness of its vision and of its human values, still survived in the chosen elite who now constituted the officer corps of the Reichswehr. We shall have to discuss this in more detail later.

Out of these elements, events, and impressions arose the first stormy waves which carried along Adolf Hitler's enterprise. He failed when he attempted the Munich Putsch of November 9, 1923. But in spite of economic improvement in the succeeding years, social conditions continued to be in such a turmoil and ferment that Hitler hoped that by following some new path he might yet seize power over Germany. The public stages of this path do not interest us here, but we want to take up again the deeper question of the transformation in the German people that eventually made his triumph possible. We have seen what he found already at hand; we shall now see how the German people, under the influence of careful methods ever more consciously and successfully applied, developed into the degenerate new-German people of Hitler's time.

5 HOMO SAPIENS AND HOMO FABER

A sound, natural, and harmonious relationship between the rational and the irrational forces of life is all important for men of modern culture and civilization. For it is precisely modern culture and civilization which by its peculiar character threatens this equilibrium. Speaking very summarily, but adequately for our purpose, we mean by rational the forces of understanding and reason and by irrational the forces of feeling, phantasy, craving, and desire. In the end reason, the rational forces, should dominate the whole surging play of the mind. But reason itself, to reach its highest and best, must also nourish itself upon irrational forces. Feeling must guide the way to the good, to the curbing of selfishness, to all moral and religious purposes; phantasy must guide the way to beauty and to the freeing of the mind from egoistically inclined desires. Feeling and phantasy together must also aid the reason in its task of comprehending the world; they must nourish and direct — with tact, restraint, and without compulsion — the impulse for knowledge and truth. The will, which in all these fields of the good, the true, and the beautiful serves as the ultimate executive power, owes obedience to Queen Reason, the mistress of all the spiritual forces springing from the whole, moulding, harmonizing, and guiding them. Any one-sided development of either the rational or the irrational forces threatens to unbalance the whole, and can eventually, if carried further and further, lead to catastrophes for the individual and for the masses, even for a whole nation, if the storm of events drives the nation in a dangerous direction.

Such a storm swept over all the German people at this time, and very few fully withstood it. Here, however, we want to discuss only those disturbances of equilibrium which came to light in Hitler's Germany.

It should be clear that the great systems of political and cultural tendencies, as they have followed one another historically and determined the attitude and activities of men, are closely connected with the proper balance of mind and spirit. Every new constellation of ideas that has inspired men leads to or springs from a new proportioning and blending of the spiritual forces. But plenty of room is left for nuances. For instance, in looking at the change from the rationalistic Enlightenment to emotional Romanticism, we may easily overlook basic characteristics, but the picture of the inner alterations in the individual man which accompany this change may be infinitely rich. Such a wealth of nuances we should perhaps expect to find in the origins of the new-German, degenerate people of the Hitler period. But we should perhaps find also among those who followed Hitler or were influenced by him a good deal that in its main tendency and spiritual structure really has other origins. We shall limit ourselves here mainly to what is typical in the origins of the people of Hitler's Germany.

The synthesis of power and spirit of the classical liberals had rested on a particularly delicate and sympathetic blending, varying in individual cases, of rational and irrational forces. The penetrating influences of modern civilization, however, were not favorable to the maintenance of a stable equilibrium between rational and irrational forces. The form of modern professional life especially has resulted in stamping a mechanistic character on life, in normalizing the aims of life, and in lessening the spontaneity of the spirit. Think, for example, of the elaboration of the system of training and examination for professional positions in the public service. The rational calculation of what is helpful, on the basis of what is officially prescribed, supersedes the free inclinations which are nourished by the spirit.

This is only one example among many of the way in which superficial rationalization can lead to an inner injury to the spirit. One must examine and throw light on these things in all their proper connections. An especially typical case which a good observer called to my attention some years ago may be mentioned here because it helps one to understand certain frequently recurring traits in the German people during the Hitler era.

It often happens nowadays, this observer said in the days before the Third Reich, that young technicians, engineers, and so forth, who have enjoyed an excellent university training as specialists, will completely devote themselves to their calling for ten or fifteen years and without looking either to the right or the left will try only to be first-rate specialists. But then, in their middle or late thirties, something they have never felt before awakens in them, something that was never really brought to their attention in their education — something that we could call a suppressed metaphysical desire. Then they rashly seize upon any sort of ideas and activities, anything that is fashionable at the moment and seems to them important for the welfare of individuals — whether it be anti-alcoholism, agricultural reform, eugenics, or the occult sciences. The former first-rate specialist changes into a kind of prophet, into an enthusiast, perhaps even into a fanatic and monomaniac. Thus arises the type of man who wants to reform the world.

Here one sees how a one-sided training of the intellect in technical work may lead to a violent reaction of the neglected irrational impulses of the spirit, but not to a real harmony of critical self-discipline and inner creativeness — rather to a new one-sidedness that clutches about wildly and intemperately.

In many of the Nazi leaders we believe we can recognize this type. Alfred Rosenberg, for instance, started as a technician and then plunged into that wild historical-philosophical complex of ideas which he proclaimed to the world in *Der Mythus des 20. Jahrhunderts* (The Myth of the Twentieth Century). A technical calling, however, does not necessarily precede the world reformer's intemperance. Men with hot heads, ambition, and an autodidactic urge for advancement, when forced into the technically normalized working conditions of the present day, may easily lose their inner equilibrium in the conflict of the spirit with the world about them and flare up in a blaze. The petty painter and aquarellist Hitler, who once had to earn his scanty bread in construction work and in the course of it whipped up his hatred of the Jews into a general philosophy (*Weltanschauung*) of world-shaking consequences, is a case of this kind.

Technology's expansion into all walks of practical life has in general called into existence a great number of new crafts and careers. It thereby finally created a new social class whose psychological structure is markedly different from that of previous social classes, both those of the old agrarian state and those of the new bourgeoisie which has blossomed out of the agrarian state. An intellect sharply concentrated upon whatever was utilitarian and immediately serviceable took possession of mental life. Through it great things could be achieved, resulting in an astonishing progress in civilization. Man's other spiritual forces, so far as they were not suppressed, avenged themselves either by those wild reactions just mentioned or fell into a general decay and debility. Feeling and phantasy, as it were, had the choice between running wild or withering. Generally they did the latter. The craving of the senses, indestructible as it is and always will be in man, received as a result of the progress of technology and civilization an abundance of new objects towards which it could direct itself. The will, as a result of the fabulous possibilities now being made attainable in practical life through the calculating and planning intellect, received a powerful stimulus and upsurge. Indeed, the later nineteenth and the twentieth centuries have truly not been lacking in tremendous energies. The calculating intellect aimed more at practical activities than at spiritual understanding. It combined with a concentrated will-power, stormed from one ostensible tremendous task to another, and only paused momentarily for relief in the material pleasures of life. Such in general outline is the picture offered by the genius of the century, a very different picture from that of the decaying late Roman Empire with which people have often compared our era.

Meanwhile, let us put aside this problem of historical comparisons and now ask ourselves instead what became of Queen Reason, that rational and superrational mistress and friend of all the other mental forces, in the course of these great alterations in spiritual life. Naturally we do not mean the prosy, dry Governess Reason of the old rationalism, but the reason of which Goethe speaks in his testament:

"Let Reason everywhere there preside
Where Life takes joy in life."

This higher reason of Goethe's day, which the syntheses of classical liberalism had achieved, did not fare well in the advancing technological age. *Homo sapiens* was supplanted by *homo faber*. No longer was there a striving for a harmony of the various mental and spiritual forces with an opportunity for their balanced expansion and development. There was only a one-sided, exaggerated peak-production of one force at the expense of the other. Even when the technological man now spoke of "reason" — and how often were we Germans to hear the word "reason" from Hitler's lips — he meant by it merely the demands put forth by a new Triple Alliance of calculating intellect, go-getting energy, and hybrid metaphysics.

There was something else that was superior to reason — the peace of God, religion. This was no specific spiritual force, but a spiritual need springing from and existing for the totality of the soul, and called upon to preserve the inner community of life of men and to knit the ties between the simple workingman and the cultured man of developed individuality. Religion likewise did not fare well in the technological age. It was crowded from its rightful position at the center of life to the periphery and was either abandoned with indifference as an outgrown and superfluous resource of earlier times or was kept in use and correspondingly honored as a useful convention and police measure for preserving quiet and order among the lower classes. Whatever still survived of genuine religion sought refuge either in the souls of individuals or among the villages and the quiet groups in the rural districts. Such groups continued to form themselves within the official church parishes. The Catholic church, with its secular arrangements, here found it easier to dispense light and warmth equally among its adherents than did the Protestants.

The truly devout and faithful were the least touched by the injurious effects of the new technological-utilitarian spirit. They continued to live their Christianity regardless of time, as their father and forefathers had lived it. How the Hitler movement attacked and fought against religion and the churches and what the task is that religion now faces after the collapse of Hitlerism will be discussed later.

6 MILITARISM AND HITLERISM

The modern technological-militarist spirit, whose connection with the people of Hitler's Germany we have just been discussing, had a prototype nearly two centuries earlier in the Prussian militarism created by Frederick William I — a fact never hitherto noticed, so far as we know. This prototype, which we have already mentioned, stamped itself extraordinarily firmly and deeply upon men. A type of Prussian officer arose who was sharply differentiated from the officer type of other countries as well as from the other professional types of his own country. The decisive factor in the development of this type was that a definitely rational concept acquired absolute dominion over all irrational elements in men. This was the concept of unconditional devotion, looking neither to right nor left, to the military profession and to the Supreme War Lord who conferred appointment to it. This devotion aimed to call forth the greatest possible professional efficiency on the parade ground as well as on the battlefield — and on the parade ground with a specially calculated system and technique. For it was there that the man was drilled, that is, made into the kind of being who was to learn how to sacrifice his life blindly for a goal not set by himself. It was here that he became one of the countless cogs and wheels in the great machine which was intended not only to sweep like thunder and lightning over the battlefield but also to produce through long years of preparation great results as a mechanical work of art serving the state's power. The military machine was regarded as an end in itself before which everything in the state must bow.

This account, at first sight, is a somewhat one-sided picture of Prussian militarism as it developed in the eighteenth century at the time of conscripted soldiers, cantonal obligations, and Regular Army tactics. For even with means which were exclusively mechanical, this artistic mechanism constructed out of human beings could not be made wholly efficient. In the Prussian officer there survived the old mediaeval sentiments of knightly service and of the loyalty of the vassal to his lord; and in the conscripted cantonist there survived a love of home and a patriarchal loyalty to the king which might become moral feathersprings of action. But with officers as well as with rank and file the mental and spiritual life as a whole remained tied tightly with and directed toward the rational aim of the greatest possible military efficiency. Strong characters, indeed, could rise to human greatness under this form of life, and mighty upheavals like those after the French Revolution and during the Goethe period added fresh new blood from the irrational realms of the spirit. Something also of the mechanical soldiery and drill spirit of Frederick William I's days continued to persist in the army based on universal military service as reorganized by Scharnhorst and Boyen. After 1815 Boyen was able with only very limited success to establish his freer, more humane, though frankly less efficient, militia (*Land-wehr*) idea in the face of the stern and exclusive spirit of the Regular Army military men. In the reorganization by King William I and Roon of the Prussian army which fought and won the wars of German unification, the Regular Army principle triumphed really for the first time. From then on, up to the two World Wars, it maintained itself as a continuum, always newly adapting itself to the times.

Furthermore, the new machine-fostered technological-utilitarian spirit of the nineteenth century met with something of a very kindred nature in the shape of the Prussian army already perfected by an earlier technique. The process of its rationalization could now proceed further with that special scientific thoroughness which the nineteenth century was again teaching. The slogan arose: "Weapons are a science; science is a weapon." Along with this strong characters of historical greatness again appeared and enrichment through finer spiritual elements was added. And so within Prussian-German militarism a key organization evolved in which all the useful characteristics of this militarism were concentrated and nurtured, so to speak, in pure form: this key organization was the Great General Staff. In it the scientific spirit, rationalism, and energy were allied. It had such vigor of life and stamped itself so deeply on the type of men created by it that it survived the Versailles Peace, which was supposed to destroy it, by means of camouflaged institutions — such as the Reich Archives, in which the history of the World War was studied by former General Staff Officers. So it was possible to fill the hundred-thousand-man Reichswehr with the spirit of this General Staff, and in turn this Reichswehr organization, with its men trained to form an officer-corps, was able to call into life the giant army of the Second World War and to create for it a General Staff which carried forward the traditions of the former staff. Not without reason did the sharp eye of our enemies detect in this General Staff the quintessence of our militarism and make it their task to extirpate it, root and branch.

However efficient this Prussian-German militarism which culminated in the General Staff proved itself to the very end to be, its efficiency was achieved through a dangerous one-sidedness. This disturbed the balance between rational and irrational motives. The purely military objective stood uppermost in its thinking and wishing. That war and the military system ought not to become ends in themselves but should remain functional servants of the total life of a nation, and not only of one nation but of the family of nations — that may perhaps have been recognized in theory by the wisest heads in the General Staff, but in practice it fell into the background in General Staff thinking. The General Staff was deficient in the necessary complementary political thinking, and its political thinking remained sound only so long as it kept in contact with the whole cultural life of the nation. But these contacts and connections between the different members of the body-politic as a whole became looser in the decades preceding the First World War. A good example of this is seen in the Schlieffen Plan. By their enormous exaggeration of purely strategic considerations the authors of the Schlieffen Plan overlooked what might be the political consequences of a German march through Belgium — consequences which in working further and further politically might change even the military situation. Here also *homo sapiens* was supplanted by *homo faber*.

The balance between rational and irrational motives, we have said, was disturbed in part by overemphasis on the technical-rational. No one, however, could deny that these General Staff officers who applied themselves intensively to exhausting work were also guided by emotional motives such as strong ambition, a high sense of duty, and a genuine patriotism. Yet one cannot be wholly happy in contemplating them. A full understanding of the totality of historical existence was lacking in these technicians of war. Therefore they could commit fatal blunders in their estimation of such matters as lay beyond the grasp of technical-military comprehension.

A serious error of this kind was made by a great part of the General Staff and the Officer Corps, transplanted into the Reichswehr, when as early as the twenties they began to look sympathetically upon Hitler's rising star. They were blinded by the semblance of the exceedingly strong national energy shining forth from the Hitler movement. One must not forget that the movement at first was only one particularly strong channel along with other similar popular movements into which people unloaded despairingly and defiantly their feelings against the Versailles peace. The thousands of dismissed officers were not the only people in whom the ferment was working. The Reichswehr, as we know, was skirted by a fringe of illegal gangs. The Putsch attempts of the year 1923 had failed, to be sure, but the same illegal spirit flared up again at every new depression in public life. Then came the serious economic crisis and the frightful unemployment of the late twenties and early thirties, when the Hitler movement grew tremendously and its relations with the Reichswehr entered an acute new stage.

After National Socialism's great successes in the elections of September 1930, the legal prosecution of young Reichswehr officers at Ulm showed how susceptible this social class was to Hitler's propaganda. About this time, not without anxiety, I asked a colonel in close touch with the Ministry of Defense about the general attitude of the Reichswehr. He assumed a reflective air and answered: "The Reichswehr will always stand where there are the strongest national interests." Several years later, when the sun of the Third Reich shone upon the Reichswehr and rearmament had begun, this same officer, who had meanwhile become a general, reminded me with a triumphant air of the answer he had given me. I was better pleased with words which I heard some time between 1930 and 1932 from the lips of Minister of Defense Groener: "It is a complete mistake to ask where the Reichswehr stands. The Reichswehr does what it is ordered to do and that's that!" At that time I too did not doubt that the Reichswehr, if employed under the authority of a President like Hindenburg against the Hitler movement in a serious situation, would do its duty in spite of its active sympathies for Hitler, just as it had done its duty a decade earlier. But these sympathies really undermined more and more the Reichswehr's respect for the constitution drawn up by a popular majority at Weimar. And did one not see that the democratically minded majority was now melting away more and more under the hot blast of the Hitler movement? We must now cast a glance at this.

An intoxication seized upon German youth at this time, both upon those who had borne arms in the World War and upon those who had grown up under the debilitating effects of the Versailles peace. On the material side they craved employment, an income, and opportunities for advancement. In the field of ideas they craved something which gave play to feelings and phantasy — to ideals which were worth living for. The Weimar Republic, to be sure, was founded on a great ideal, for which a whole politically ripe nation ought to have lived and fought — the ideal of an established national community uniting both working class and bourgeoisie, the ideal that all groups formerly avowedly hostile to the state should be permeated by a sound national feeling, not exaggerated but embracing all human values. Combined with this ideal in the Weimar majority was the firm determination to throw off, or at least to loosen, one by one the fetters of the Versailles Treaty, by working patiently and slowly through steady though meagre compromises with the victorious powers. It was at that time the only politically realistic method possible for gradually doing away with the restrictions. Every other method threatened sooner or later to lead to war, and every war to lead again, as happened later, to a catastrophe for Germany.

Such a program, however, involved much too much reasonableness and resignation on the part of the craving youth of 1930. "You have offered us no ideals," they cried out against the Weimar supporters; "you cannot fully satisfy us" — and they meant it, as we said, in both the material and the ideological sense. There is a natural impulse in all youth to form associations which stimulate impulses for speedy action wherever possible. So in the early thirties many young people, worthy but wholly unripe politically, began to organize themselves as the Storm Troops (SA, *Sturmabteilungen*) of the Hitler movement. Hitler, one may say, came to power through a typical but dazzled and blinded youth movement.

"It would be a pity to have to fire on these splendid youths," was now the saying in the Reichswehr's ranks. I repeated this saying to Groener, and he replied scoffingly: "As if there were not a great many worthy youths in the other camp also!" These youths, however, were not so highly inflamed as those in the Hitler camp.

So we return to the currents within the Reichswehr and come to the strongest material motive in the Reichswehr's growing friendliness toward the Hitler movement. "We shall create for you a great army, much larger than you yourselves imagine today," it was intimated in the ranks of the Hitler youth. What a dazzling prospect of quick promotion and breathing space in life for the Officer Corps of the hundred-thousand-man army! And also for the masses of former officers who had been dismissed and were now having a hard time in life!

The restoration of universal military service, a heritage from the War of Liberation, could also be a high ideal for those who disliked the Hitler movement. However, as the historical situation then stood, it could and must be only a universal military service without specific militarism — therefore some kind of militia, something similar to the Swiss type. Temperate statesmen, who at the same time were moved by deep national sentiment, like Brüning and Groener, now believed it possible to secure such a militia through negotiations with the victor powers. The plan was, so Groener told me later, to leave the Reichswehr practically as it stood, except for some increase in the matter of heavy armament, and alongside of it to create on the basis of universal military service "frontier defense divisions" made up of new recruits and men with a half-year training, up to a strength of about two hundred thousand men. "We approached England and Italy with this plan and secured their approval in principle. We were on the point of approaching France — and then came our dismissal." (The Brüning Cabinet, to which Groener had belonged, fell May 30, 1932.)

We shall hear later of other very promising plans of Brüning and his colleagues. In this case of the proposed militia system one must note that there was the possibility that Brüning and Groener might have succeeded in taking the wind out of the sails of the swelling Hitler movement by making a valuable gain of national importance. Then Germany and Europe would have been spared the catastrophe of the Second World War. To be sure, who can say definitely that this possibility could have become a reality? Here — exactly as in the case of many turning points in world history where a fortunate possibility was neglected and an unfortunate reality was adopted — is a problematical question which keeps ringing softly but insistently in one's ear.

On the Reichswehr, however, on its attitude, feeling, and inclination, depended primarily the fate of Germany and therewith of Europe, according to my conviction. It held in its hand the balance of power in the state. It should not and would not have intervened directly upon its own decision, but it would have hearkened in the last resort to a command of the President of the Republic. Between the President, who was at the same time a field marshal, and the Reichswehr there existed relations of mutual dependence. The Reichswehr obeyed him, but he listened to it. He absorbed into his mind and spirit everything to which it was sensitive. He was flesh and blood of its flesh and blood, a genuine off-shoot of that Prussian-German militarism which had produced so many first-rate technical and so few politically far-seeing heads. It was not that in his own decisions he wanted to follow directly the wishes of the Reichswehr; the relationship was not so simple as that. He had hearkened to the voice of statesmanlike reason for a long time; then, becoming deaf to it, he sent for Hitler. If one probes psychologically to the deepest and most basic reason that brought him to this decision, it can be nothing else but Prussian-German militarism. This militarism can be regarded as the historical force which certainly helped forward most strongly the building up of the Third Reich.

Some freer characters with finer political feeling and humane culture, who carried forward the traditions of Scharnhorst, Gneisenau, and Boyen, still always managed to lift themselves out of this ordinarily narrow militarism. Among them were Defense Minister, later Interior Minister, Groener and Major General Hans von Haeften, who was then President of the Reich Archives and directed its historical war studies. I had the good fortune to stand on a friendly footing with both men and met them often. Even in these two men, who thoroughly disliked the Hitler movement, I observed with increasing anxiety in the winter of 1931–32 the development of a fatalistic attitude of mind. "I see the flood rising ever higher and higher; we shall not be able to stop it," Haeften once exclaimed to me in profound agitation. Groener thought of compromising with it and calling individual National Socialists to join the government. He also received Hitler once and allowed himself to be deluged with his torrent of talk. As he told me later, Hitler gazed fixedly at the ceiling and preached about Buddha and Confucius. Later, after his own fall, Groener recognized, I believe, that such impulses to come to an understanding with Hitler were a mistake. On one of our walks together he once stood still, struck his cane on the ground, and exclaimed: "We ought to have suppressed them by force." I agreed with him with complete conviction, since I had long recognized the depth of the abyss between the Hitler spirit and the sound German spirit. Where it was a question of Germany's whole future, of her political, spiritual, and moral health, a life-and-death struggle ought to have been risked.

Groener, to be sure, at that time was sick, suffering from diabetes, a fact which is not to be wholly overlooked. This illness, perhaps, restricted his full energy. He also stood, I suspect, somewhat strongly under the influence of his chief colleague in the Defense Ministry, the head-strong and intriguing General von Schleicher. He was another case, with special nuances, taken from Prussian-German militarism and the General Staff. As a General Staff officer in the First World War, Schleicher had had a tendency to undertake more than mere General Staff work — to be active as a political figure and by clever advice to manage men and affairs from behind the scenes. (Ludwig Bernhard, who knew a good deal, once told me that Groener's appointment to Supreme Command in the army as Ludendorff's successor in October 1918 was made as a result of Schleicher's advice.) Schleicher's manner reminded one of Privy Councillor Fritz von Holstein, the hidden managing demon of German policy under Bülow. As a political figure, however, Schleicher felt himself to have an elective affinity with the great men of practical politics (*Realpolitik*), with the genius of Machiavelli and of Bismarck. He looked at political life as a game of calculable forces which one could manage by superior skill to the advantage of his own country, if he kept himself free from prejudices and party dogmas. Flexibility was to him a main point. He realized the harmfulness of National Socialism and he apparently never thought of handing over the fate of the whole state to it. But this did not exclude for him the possibility of partially exploiting it for the benefit of the Reichswehr and the government. He believed also that he could guide the wild waves of the tempest into safe channels by means of clever and well-measured concessions. He acted accordingly later, when he entered Papen's Government. Before this, however, in the spring of 1932, during Groener's administration of the Ministry of Defense, he executed a complete change of front within a very short time. I follow here Groener's account. According to this, Schleicher at first favored and supported Groener's intention of finally dealing an energetic blow against the Hitler movement, and so on April 13 the Hitler Storm Troops and Elite Guard

(SA and SS) were outlawed. "It was high time that this was done, and it was fortunate that it was done," Groener said to me at the time. But when Groener had to defend the prohibition of the SA in the Reichstag on May 10 and did so very awkwardly and lamely because of a bad turn in his health, thereby disappointing many of the deputies, Schleicher suddenly turned about within twenty-four hours and declared the prohibition to be impracticable. Thus he struck his minister from behind and thereby possibly decided the downfall of the Brüning-Groener government. His own experiments as Groener's successor, and later as short-lived Reich Chancellor, plunged him also into the pit he had dug for Groener. His final fate of being murdered by the Nazis on June 30, 1934, is well known.

Let us return to our purpose of elucidating the universal-historical aspect of the connections between militarism and Hitlerism. *Exercitus facit imperatorem* is an old and important saying. It does not mean merely that the army chooses the ruler in the manner of the Roman Praetorians. It means also that in some often hidden way, not to be formally grasped, the rule at any given time in the state depends essentially upon the disposition and will of its armed branch. The ideal aim, to be sure, of the healthy state is that on the contrary the armed branch shall remain merely the executive organ of the will of the ruler. But historical experience shows that there is a fundamental and mutual interaction between the state and its armed branch and that the state's aims are profoundly influenced by the character of the military system. Thus, the fate of the Hitler movement at this time depended to a high degree upon the attitude and disposition of the Reichswehr. No one presumably knew this better than Hitler himself. He succeeded in no small degree in dazzling the Reichswehr and enticing it over to his support. The lack of understanding in Reichswehr circles as to the national worth of the Hitler movement was in turn closely connected with the one-sidedness in Prussian-German militarism, with its highly developed technical spirit and drilling of mere military specialists. The result was a very inadequate understanding on the part of the Reichswehr of all the other forces of life in Germany and consequently a very deficient circulation of healthy blood throughout the whole of the German social organism. The counterinfluence of the Scharnhorst-Boyen spirit was never able to register more than a very limited success. And the attempt of a finessing general like Schleicher to grasp the spokes of fortune's wheel by means of a poor imitation of Bismarck's *Realpolitik* was in the end completely abortive.

The Reichswehr received from Hitler a fulfillment of the promises that he had made to it. The enlargement of the army and the rearmament began. But the hope perhaps indulged in by many a Reichswehr general that the saying *exercitus facit imperatorem* would also be verified and that the Reichswehr and not Hitler would have the last word to say in the Third Reich were not to be fulfilled. On the contrary, slowly, shrewdly, step by step, the party won the spiritual domination over the army. This process was admirably portrayed in Rauschning's *The Revolution of Nihilism* which was published abroad before the Second World War, and can be regarded as a good warning to the German officer class not to degenerate into freebooting leaders (*Landesknechtsführer*) in the service of Hitler's party. When the party got so far that it no longer needed to fear the old army and the traditions still alive in it, Himmler brought something further to pass — the formation of a new army nucleus created wholly by the party but cleverly dispersed through the units of the old regular army: the Heavy Armed Elite Guards (*Waffen*-SS). And now the meaning of the saying *exercitus facit imperatorem* took on new life. The spirit, or rather the evil spirit, of the *Waffen*-SS determined henceforth the character and aims of the ruling authorities and led us into the abyss.

7 MASS MACHIAVELLISM

As we have already explained, the character of the German people of Hitler's day resulted from a continuous shifting since Goethe's time of psychological forces — a disturbing of the psychological equilibrium between the rational and the irrational. The calculating intellect was excessively exaggerated on the one hand, and the emotional desire for power, wealth, security, and so forth on the other hand. As a result the acting will power was driven onto dangerous ground. Whatever could be calculated and achieved technically, if it brought wealth and power, seemed justified — in fact, even morally justified, if it served the welfare of one's own country. The new ethics of national egoism, the doctrine of *sacro egoismo,* had to be added to give this shifting of the psychological forces the proper blessing. Men now began to think about these conflicts between new and old ethics in Machiavellian terms, or at least were influenced toward Machiavellism. For the German people of the Third Reich there finally came to be no conflict between various ethical laws at all, but only the single law: "Win power at any price!"

For propaganda, to be sure, some support from the other older ethics was needed. This was found in the slogan, "Common welfare takes precedence over individual welfare" (*Gemeinnutz geht vor Eigennutz*). If one now considers the last monstrous performance of the Hitler party as it finally left the scene — the heroic determination to survive by means of a truly unscrupulous and ruinous exploitation of the people's last drop of strength in order to lengthen a little the life of the bankrupt concern — then one sees at once that the welfare of the party and its leaders had swallowed up in itself the common welfare of the German people.

The phrase coined in Italy, *sacro egoismo,* certainly indicates that it was not only in Germany that there were shifting changes in spiritual and intellectual life. "Our country, right or wrong!" was the saying of the American Jingo. The phrase, if given absolute acceptance, is hideous and harmful in its consequences, because it throws aside all moral limits in political transactions. And certainly it was not accepted in the absolute sense as a maxim of English or American policy. But, as I once had occasion to show, it is in the very nature of *Staatsräson* or *raison d'état*, and of state guidance in general, that something demonic lies which at a given moment leaps up and seizes control over the ruling authorities. *Raison d'état* and Machiavellism are general and eternal human phenomena. But they become stronger and all at once explode tremendously at definite times in history and in definite nations that are inclined that way. The difference in situation between the times and nations of today and those of the *ancien régime* from the Italian Renaissance onwards is that formerly the *ragione di stato* and Machiavellism were the more or less secretly guarded province of a small class of political thinkers and statesmen. They lived in the midst of people who received their moral teaching from the Church and otherwise lived naïvely and unreflectively amid the needs and narrowness of their daily life. Formerly intellectual culture was also an affair of the few who could develop it very intensively and successfully. That was the thoroughly aristocratic character of the *ancien régime* to which a man like Burckhardt always looked back with longing, for meanwhile the era of the masses and of whole peoples awakened to self-consciousness has arrived.

The basic dynamic force of the past century and a half, the enormous increase in population which by its pressure has called forth wholly new historical phenomena, here again comes to light. Politics is now no longer the affair of the few; ever larger classes, pushing up from below, want to take a hand in it. And this widening of the circle of politically active people multiplies the keys to the chest of poisons in which lie the essences of Machiavellism. From being an aristocratic affair, Machiavellism became a bourgeois affair, and finally became mass Machiavellism. It had already arrived in the age of imperialism before the First World War.

Every political leader participating in it could justify ethically his often rude folk-egoism by his intense solicitude for the life and existence of his own people. He could appear very noble and great if he took up the really frightful phrase, "my country, right or wrong," and acted accordingly.

No, the Machiavellian, amoral element in the Germans of Hitler's day was not limited to Germany alone but was part of the general fermentation in a monstrous process, whether of the decline or of the transformation of the West into new forms of life. "There is none who doeth good, no, not one," can be thrown back in answer to those who accuse the German people of disturbing the peace of nations by its amoral, intoxicated craze for power.

This truth, however, ought not to be a justification for us Germans. When the universal Occidental character of the evil has once been recognized, ethical as well as historical considerations demand that we Germans should mind our own business and seek to understand Germany's special part in it. For in the end may not the accusation of our opponents be correct to the extent that, though we were not the only ones, we have produced in the shape of the Germans of the Third Reich the mass Machiavellism which is perhaps the most dangerous for the world? This question will often occupy us. Must we not always be shocked at the precipitous fall from the heights of the Goethe era to the swamps of the Hitler period? Passionately we Germans ask ourselves how this was possible within the selfsame nation. We are reminded of Grillparzer's mid-nineteenth-century words, which are both a diagnosis and a prognosis: "Humanity — Nationality — Bestiality." But these words still do not give us a complete answer to our question. Only the general picture of a development which leads from the culture of the few to the unculture of the masses can explain it. It cannot be explained by the individual peculiarities of the German development, nor even by the unique historical circumstances, events, and decisions which at clear and definite points have perhaps definitely determined its course. Let us try to say at least a little about it.

Peculiar to the German mentality, as we have already indicated, was the often stormy inclination to rise up suddenly from the limitations of the reality which surrounded it and perhaps more strongly moved it, enticed it, and tormented it than was the case with other peoples — the inclination to soar up suddenly into the limitless, into a metaphysical or at times merely quasi-metaphysical world, which was supposed to emancipate it. This inclination reached a high point in Luther as well as in Goethe's time and in German idealism, even in Hegel's idealism. Suppose, however, that the limitless should be sought in the physical world and was regarded as something inherent and immanent in it, and that it was through reality itself that the ways and means were to be found for disentangling tangles and for escaping from limitations. That happened after the middle of the nineteenth century through everything that men called reality, realism, *Realpolitik,* and so forth, and that glorified the new leaders in their actions. Thereby, as they thought, men had again conquered the limitless. Thus the old metaphysical inclination of the German mentality manifested itself once again, but by error and perversion did not conquer any really metaphysical realm for itself, but simply treated an earthly realm as if it were a metaphysical one or at least nearly so. Thus, even Treitschke, although he was quite at home in a genuine metaphysical realm, could make the serious assertion that the essence of the state is power, and again power, and for a third time power. Power, to be sure, belongs to the essence of the state, but never embodies it exclusively without emptying it of its ethical content. Treitschke's uncritical assertion contributed much to the development in the German bourgeoisie of the intoxicated craze for power.

It is here a question not so much of an accusation as of an understanding, of an exploratory examination of an initially sound and organic life process, in order to discover the points where lay the first tendencies to hypertrophy and degeneration which were at last frightfully evident to us. Sound and organically deeply necessary was the turning of the German spirit toward reality, at first quite slowly after

1815, then more strongly after 1830. Thoroughly sound also at that time was the awakening desire for national unity and for a national power-state of the kind at first bound up with the heritage of the Goethe period in those syntheses of classical liberalism that we have dealt with earlier. Unique events, decisions, and acts, however, then shifted the main emphasis in these syntheses and programs of the nationalist bourgeoisie more and more in the direction of earthly realism and power politics; thus these shifts fundamentally determined the character of the work of national unification. Had there been success — or rather let us cautiously say, could there have been any success at all — in winning national unity by means of the Frankfurt National Assembly of 1848–49, then the whole German development would have taken place in much closer contact with western European development than actually occurred. The ideals of the German National Union of 1859 still evidenced close feeling with the liberal ideas of western Europe. But the steering of the work of national unification was transferred from the hands of the unarmed professors and the equally unarmed writers and economists of 1859 to the hands of an arms-minded Junker, Otto von Bismarck. The specifically Prussian and militarist characteristics of which we have already spoken were stamped upon him. Perhaps it would not have been at all possible to win for Germany a closer unity, with its political power secured, in any other way. And it was a way which was possible only in Germany and nowhere else. People could pride themselves on the fact that national unity had been achieved in a manner distinctively German, and not according to western European formulas. But a decisive deviation from western European liberal ideas had not resulted. It is known how Crown Prince Frederick William, and still more his English wife, followed with sorrow this course of events. So the year 1866, just as was felt by Burckhardt, Constantin Frantz, and Planck, was a year of destiny of the first order for Germany and for Europe. It was a year of destiny in a much deeper sense than we Germans generally, prior to the World Wars, had been accustomed to regard it.

Once more we must repeat that it is here not a question of accusing, but of understanding. Bismarck's founding of the German Empire was an achievement of historic greatness, and the enthusiastic reception which we who grew up with it gave it remains for us a precious memory. But today we must admit that formerly, in the brilliance of the achievement, we saw too little the hidden, dark points where it was vulnerable and where disease might later set in. The Empire gave too much play to Prussian militarism and with it to that dangerous mentality of Prussian self-sufficiency which it could create or foster in the Empire's leaders and in the bourgeoisie. Thereby the path to mass Machiavellism became broader in Germany. The break with the Goethe period and its ideal of humanity became surprisingly sharp. As the shrewd observer Carl Hillebrand once wrote in the 1870's, to read today the letters and diaries of Goethe's era seems as though we are already separated from it not by decades but by centuries.

However, in spite of all sorts of cracks and flaws in the joints (*Kulturkampf*, Social Democratic Party), there was still such a sound balance of forces and so much joyous, creative energy of life in the leaders and the led, that we cannot say that there was any complete degeneration before the First World War. If Bismarck's caution and wise circumspection had been exercised by his successors in European and world policy, we should have passed through the danger zone of the age of imperialism and perhaps also have been able to get ahead with the curing of our internal ills.

8 CHANCE AND GENERAL TENDENCIES

Chance, once wrote Justi in his life of Winckelmann, plays a role in history, a much greater role than the philosophers of history imagine. Chance in history may be defined as that which does not arise from a general and overpowering necessity, but from a unique and unexpected intervention of some sort of extraneous factor in the course of history. We go back to the end of the last chapter and ask whether William II cannot be called an unfortunate example of chance in German history. Because with another ruler in his place, perhaps one of only average ability but who corresponded in character more to the beneficent Hohenzollern type, everything would have gone differently and more happily. This possibility cannot be denied, but it must at once be supplemented by a glance at the general tendencies which also accompanied the chance fact of William II. There were those degenerative developments in the German bourgeoisie and other classes and those inherent evils of Prussian militarism, of which we spoke, which emerged in the personality of William II as an individual. Who can clearly and completely separate the chance personality from the general tendencies which rise from the depths of the life of the people?

In the relationship between the chance personality and the general tendencies there are endless variations. Quickly they become more separate but never completely separate; quickly they melt inseparably together. Now one factor is stronger, and now the other. Sometimes things seem necessarily to run their course in such a way that nothing at all depends on the individual. But then again an individual intervenes with monstrous vehemence of effect. In everything we may call chance there lies something of the general tendency, and in every general tendency something of chance. In the course of the First World War and in the necessary creation of the Weimar Republic general forces were dominant — for the most part any of the individuals who were here active could have been replaced by someone else who would have done about the same thing. But then came the monstrous effect of Hitler's personality upon already existing general tendencies, which consequently increased enormously and could almost be regarded as his most personal creation. The general tendencies existed in the shape of the currents of rage and despair, and often also the wild readiness for action, which, when Hitler appeared, were already welling up in all classes discontented with the Weimar creation. He needed various fighting aims of a general character to which he could point and through which he could raise to the boiling point the blood of his followers. These aims were the Versailles Treaty and the conditions created by it, then the Jewish question, and finally the economic crisis and unemployment of the late twenties. Without the preëxistence of these three complexes Hitler's influence would have been incomprehensible. In a period of quiet the seriously psychopathic individual and the unsuccessful artist would probably have lived his problematical existence to one side somewhere or other. But upon the stage of history the times which were out of joint excited the personality that was out of joint to a mutual and most fearful degree.

It is not necessary here, and it would go against my grain, to draw a fuller character sketch of the unholy man. I shall only cite two observations, which I heard from others, because they touch the central point to be considered concerning Hitler's place in German history. Otto Hintze once said to me: "This fellow really does not belong to our race at all. There is something wholly foreign about him, something like an otherwise extinct primitive race that is still completely amoral in its nature." And General Beck — the same man who paid with his life on July 20, 1944, for his attempt to rid us of Hitler — told me in a conversation a long time before: "This fellow has no Fatherland at all." Both remarks confirm the true impression that in Hitler's character and actions, in spite of his very close connection with the life of his time, there lay something foreign to us Germans and difficult to understand. In any case there was something very egocentric, which with monstrous energy made use of the existing historical forces and the aspirations of his German contemporaries, but he was not really altogether integrated with them and rooted in them. Similar observations have also been made about Napoleon I. In the mightiest of the men of power in world history one very often comes upon puzzling depths where the natural connection between the self and the surrounding world is lacking or seems to be breaking apart. At any rate, the end of Hitler's life shows that at the decisive moment he was no longer concerned for the welfare of the German people or for the preservation of such of its substance as was not already destroyed. The remark is attributed to him: "If I go under, the German people also shall go under." He acted in accordance with this remark. I think there is better evidence for another remark, repeated to me as early as the spring of 1944, which he is believed to have made in the circle of his leaders: "If Providence denies victory to me, then I shall take care that the German people do not survive this disgrace."

At bottom, therefore, there was an uncanny gulf between his demonic self and the world about him which he dominated and defiled. He could indeed win to himself a circle of daring and unscrupulous adventurers and fortune hunters as a solid following, because with such an extraordinary personality at their head they could hope to come to the top. He could also fascinate wide circles of the German people and bring them to believe that in him they had found the leader who would fulfill their idealistic demands — many would say that he was the proclaimer of a new religion. But doubt as to the genuineness of what he proclaimed as an idealistic demand is aroused the moment one looks into the fundamentally egocentric character of his personality. The glorification and enthronement of his own race which he made the central point of his doctrine does not — in spite of the fervent words which he knew how to use about it in *Mein Kampf* — bear so much the character of an ideal suffusing the whole soul as the character of a monstrously effective means to power that would again be allowed to drop if a still more effective means could be found, or if it no longer seemed opportune to use it. If his belief in the world mission of the Nordic race had really been a heartfelt matter with him, he could never have concluded the alliance with Japan, which withdrew East Asia from this Nordic race and handed it over to a foreign and supposedly inferior race.

Hitler's confession of faith, therefore, does not seem to spring from any innermost spiritual need. He could have sounded another note and still have become the great successful demagogue before whom the world held its breath. In saying this we do not want to make him into a merely opportunistic calculator — although he could play at this and be very tricky, yes, deadly sly. But there was also elemental passion in his racial dogma, which he formed for himself in the overheated atmosphere of Austrian anti-Semitism. His hatred of the Jews was as honest and as monomaniacal as it was bestial. Toward the Jew, as he came to know him in the East, he had at the outset, for the first time perhaps, freed himself from traditional moral restraints and begun to think in amoral terms. This purely instinctive element in his nature was then melted together almost indistinguishably with the calculating element in the glowing fire of a wild enthusiasm. This enthusiasm, as we indicated earlier, was, to be sure, akin to the enthusiasm of those half-educated persons who, brought up at first as purely rational technicians, suddenly somersault into uncritical fanaticism — but the Hitler enthusiasm from the very outset was much more strongly a matter of his own self, of his own world mission. An old general once remarked to me: "One can see who he is by the kind of people he has chosen for his leaders; they are either rascals or fools." In Hitler the two were entangled together.

His confession of faith, his so-called *Weltanschauung,* we believe, could also have been different, and yet he still might have been able to become the dynamically powerful exploiter of his people and of the situation at the time. There was something of personal chance about it. In view of the monstrous success of Hitler's rise to power, may one not venture to question whether after all it resulted from general causes? Did not chance, fatally for Germany, weave its thread into the fabric? And precisely at the decisive points during Hitler's rise to power in the state in the years from 1930 to 1933? It is cheap wisdom to avoid this question and with gloomy fatality to explain the misfortune that Hitler brought upon Germany as an inescapable destiny. We have taken the trouble to examine Germany's past according to the course of events and the facts of a general nature that were at work prior to Hitlerism. Now it is an important fact that, at the time when the Reichstag elections were still tolerably free in 1932–33, Hitler's following never won a real majority — indeed in the second Reichstag election of 1932 it clearly fell off somewhat (from 13.7 to 11.7 million). This fact makes it impossible to pass over in silence the question whether the demon chance did not come to the aid of the daring gambler and big swindler Hitler in his rise to power and in his final call to the office of chancellor.

I shall first tell something that I heard from a well-known former leader of the German National People's Party. At a small gathering I had given a short talk about the problem of chance in history. Afterwards this man came over to me and said: "Your words remind me of June 30, 1930. At that time the German National People's Party held a decisive meeting on the question of whether or not it should support the Brüning Government. My friends and I were in favor of support; Hugenberg and his following were against it. Wholly by chance, a couple of my friends were absent from the meeting. Had they been present, the vote would have been in favor of Brüning — and the whole later course of events might have turned out differently, that is, might have turned against Hitler." But as it happened, Hugenberg won the vote and led his party to its foolhardy alliance with Hitler. And Hitler in turn, supported by such an alliance, could then present himself to President von Hindenburg as the leader of a real majority composed of two great parties.

One sees indeed from this series of events that chance was closely interwoven with general tendencies. Hugenberg's momentous decision of 1930, which allowed Hitler to become the pacemaker for the German Nationalist Party, was not made possible exclusively by the chance vote of 1930 but also by the influence which Hugenberg, as the great money dis-

penser, as the master of the conservative press, and as the busy
wire-puller in general, had exercised for years upon his party
throughout the country. And in his party likewise, from the
beginning in 1919, the strongest kind of resentment had been
fermenting against the Weimar Republic, against Social Democracy, and against the trade unions. The reactionary,
agrarian, upper bourgeois, and big-business elements which
were united in the German National People's Party were
positively determined not to reform the Weimar system in
the way that Brüning wished, but to sabotage it. The more
moderate elements in the party, however, after their chance
discomfiture on June 30, 1930, finally sought to form a new
party friendly to Brüning, the People's Conservatives. They
could make no headway, however, against the mighty influence exercised by Hugenberg through his press upon the mass
of the German National People's Party voters. Hugenberg
and Hitler concluded their alliance in the mutual hope that
one could hit the other over the head and be able to win the
final victory in the Reich for his own party. Eventually
Hugenberg was soundly punished for his blindness to the
Hitler danger, because after the successful joint final victory
in 1933 Hitler gave him and his party their walking papers.
The Moor had done his duty and could now go.

In the spring of 1934 in a small gathering I met Brüning
before he sought safety from Hitler's agents and murderers
by escape abroad. I said to him: "Germany's fate in falling
into Hitler's power depended primarily on the decisions of
two men — Hugenberg and Hindenburg." "It was exactly so,"
he replied, and he knew the course of events much more
intimately than I and was never in any way prejudiced by
purely personal views.

We come now to Hindenburg's part in Hitler's seizure of
power and to an amplification of what has already been said
in the chapter on militarism. In order to make our argument
more effective, we shall depart from a strictly chronological
account.

When at midday on January 30, 1933, the telephones everywhere in Greater Berlin, within an hour after the event, carried the news that the Reich President had just signed Hitler's appointment as Reich Chancellor, I said to myself with the deepest consternation not only that a day of misfortune of the first order had dawned for Germany but also, "This was not necessary." Here existed no pressing political or historical necessity such as had led to the downfall of William II in the autumn of 1918. Here it was no general tendency, but something like chance, specifically Hindenburg's weakness, that had turned the scales.

I know of course that this view will always be contested. But since it concerns a key problem in the downfall of Bismarckian Germany, it will in later times still have a breathless interest for thoughtful persons. Whether Hitler's appointment could have been avoided is by no means so idle a question as a banal philosophy of history might suggest. Because, according to the answer that it receives, the picture of the general psychological and political condition of the German people will appear differently — either more hopeful or more hopeless. If the question is answered in the negative, or if it is established that Hitler would have certainly come to power in some other way if not in this, then a worse light would be thrown upon the German people's power of moral resistance. The poisoning which the people had already received from Hitler, and all the secular weaknesses and defects of which we have spoken and which had been at work prior to this poisoning, would appear incurable. If everything had to happen exactly as it did happen, then also the frightful catastrophe of the war, which arose from Hitlerism and put an end to it, might enfeeble the courage to live and labor. Such a gloomy fatalism might weaken the energies of those who are called upon to lead.

That is the practical side of the problem. Its theoretical side, however, demands that the factor of freedom of action in history — that is, the possibility of being able to do otherwise than was done — must never be overlooked. If we admit this possibility of freedom in the case before us and concede that Hitler's accession to power could successfully have been prevented, then the German people's share of the responsibility for having brought Hitler to power would be less. We can now look around for arguments which might support this view.

We have already given some of these arguments in another connection. The Reichswehr, in spite of all its sympathies for Hitler, would presumably have obeyed the order of Hindenburg, that idol of the soldiery, if he had called upon it for protection from some kind of attempted violence on the part of the Hitler party. But there was no need of letting things go as far as that, because the regular police (*Schutzpolizei* or *Schupo*) already had sufficient armed means with which successfully to oppose the Nazis and also the communists, who were carrying on a simultaneous and powerful agitation. The danger from the communists was terribly exaggerated by the Nazis in order to gain votes and influence for themselves among the bourgeoisie and the ruling authorities, and so that they could recommend themselves as the saviors of the bourgeois order of society. But so far as the National Socialist movement among the masses themselves is concerned, it was on the decline, as proved by the figures already cited of the Reichstag elections of 1932. Granted, the decline was small. But the charm was broken — the notion that the movement was becoming an ever more gigantic and irresistible landslide. The Goebbels confessions also allow us to see that the leaders of the party had been seized with a strong depression of spirit in January 1933. It seemed as though they regarded the game as already lost. Then, with a mighty summoning of all their demagogic arts, they intervened in the elections for the state legislature in Lippe-Detmold and won there a solitary victory (1932 Reichstag elections in Lippe-Detmold, July 31, 42,000; November 6, 32,000; compared with the Lippe-Detmold state election, January 15, 1933, of about 30,000). It was a prestige success that resembled an attack of closely packed heavy artillery upon a solitary village. I said this at the time in an article which appeared in the democratic press two days before the Reichstag fire. It was the last tolerably free word that one still dared to utter prior to the terror which set in and closed all our lips. A statesman at the head of the government, however, if possessed of temperate judgment and a firm determination to ward off vital danger, could not have been led astray by this solitary Lippe-Detmold victory of the Nazis. No doubt, however, the men surrounding Hindenburg did their best to bring the perhaps resisting old man around to the view that the power of the Hitler movement was unbroken.

We must now go back a little in examining the question of whether the summoning of Hitler to office was unavoidable. The terrible unemployment during these years was the most effective influence that was driving despairing men into the arms of the Hitler movement. But the world economic crisis, which was the cause of it and which had lasted for several years, already showed the first small signs of improvement. I remember a conversation I had about it in the autumn of 1932 with a former Reich Economics Minister. Papen, the experimenting successor to Brüning, was Chancellor at the time. The first steps which he took seemed to be crowned with success. The man with whom I was talking observed in these very words: "Papen now has the good luck that under his administration the world economic crisis is letting up."

Brüning's fall and Papen's summons to office on June 1, 1932, was the first fatal act of yielding to the Hitler movement. With Brüning and his cabinet disappeared the men who had led the fight against Hitler with the conviction that they had to avert a vital danger from Germany. Had their fight become really so hopeless that one could understand Hindenburg's decision to abandon it and try a half concession to the Hitler movement? By no means. Shortly before this the elections for the Reich President on April 10, 1932, had resulted in a clear victory for Hindenburg over Hitler (Hindenburg over 19 million votes or 53 per cent of votes cast; Hitler over 13 million votes or 36.8 per cent of votes cast; the rest fell to the communist Thälmann). There was still therefore a grand majority among the whole people which could have been encouraged and organized from above for defense.

It would have been the job of the Brüning government to begin fighting against Hitler not merely by repressive means but also by undertaking positive measures to heal the discontent and desperation of the masses on which Hitler's movement nourished itself. Such positive measures were already in preparation when the lightning struck and Brüning was dismissed.

Most urgent were measures for creating employment. To accomplish this, large Reich credits would have to be given. Hitherto anxiety for the maintenance of the value of the paper money and for the avoidance of a new inflation had prevented this. But in the spring of 1932 Brüning decided to risk it. The Minister of Justice in his cabinet, Joël, a man of character, told me about it later. Brüning's plan was to use nearly a billion marks (800 million) for creating employment, but to wait until the first signs of a letting up of the economic crisis appeared and until the heavily oppressive reparations burden had been cast off. To spend this credit any sooner as an economic stimulus might otherwise have resulted in diluting it by inflation and have amounted, so to speak, to throwing the money out the window. Now the first signs of a let-up in the economic crisis came, as we saw, in 1932, and the decisive favorable turn in the reparations negotiations with the powers had already been reached by Brüning himself. What Brüning had prepared was reaped by his successor Papen, when he signed on July 9, 1932, after Brüning's fall, the Lausanne Agreement. This agreement practically wiped out the fearful reparations burden that had ever and again threatened Germany's credit.

There would also have been the job of taking the wind out of the sails of Hitler's party, which was declaring that it alone was capable of satisfying Germany's great national basic demands. This was not easy for a man like Brüning who, with his sense of responsibility, could not play the gambler's win-or-lose-all game, for which a man like Hitler was ready. The victor powers ought to have recognized this situation. They ought to have strengthened Brüning's position in the Reich by effective concessions, in order to avert the danger to world peace which was threatened by Hitler's seizure of power. But one can understand that the victor powers were handicapped by the suspicion that a Hitler might become the beneficiary of such concessions. They did, however, constantly make decisive concessions at this time in the reparations question. With regard to the army question, they were on the way to concede Germany's reintroduction of universal military service, as we have heard earlier. Groener also had further plans. In the party's youth organizations formed by Hitler there was embodied the pedagogical idea of having the state satisfy a natural need on the part of youth through arrangements for physical exercise and for molding the mind. Groener intended to take this molding process out of the hands of the Storm Troops and the Hitler Youth and transfer it to the veterans' organization of Steel Helmets (*Stahlhelm*) which, it was hoped, would thereby be won away from its former attitude and come into the camp of Hitler's opponents.

But did not all these things which could have taken place on the positive side proceed too slowly and hesitatingly? Did they not lack the soaring sweep of a great resolve for which the starving, excited people, and especially the clamoring youth, now longed and believed that they heard in Hitler's stormy speeches? At this very time there were persons who raised this question, some with anxiety and others with satisfaction, and doubted Brüning's and Groener's suitability for the task. I myself have already mentioned that Groener's health had suffered. But, so far as my observation goes, Groener and Brüning were by no means lacking in a firm determination to stand fast as pilots through the storm. And the favorable outcome of the election of the Reich President in the spring of 1932 gave them a very stanch standard for their fight. Shortly afterwards, when I had a visit from Groener and expressed to him my confidence in his victorious continuance of the fight, he replied in an already slightly depressed tone, "Yes, if I continue to have the confidence of the Reich President." Another time, after his fall, he said to me, "Brüning and I wanted to continue the fight, but the Old Man did not."

That was the decisive factor in the situation. Brüning and Groener, to be sure, could at first preach only reason and patience to their followers among the people, but so long as they could show no tangible successes in their policy they left unsatisfied the phantasy in men which Hitler so richly nourished. Reason and patience, however, on the part of statesmen, combined with toughness, have often in history triumphed over the irrational force of misguided public feeling.

The fact remains that Brüning and Groener were torn away from a struggle for the vital interests of the German people — a struggle which, to be sure, was not outwardly brilliant but which was painstaking and took much patience. They were torn away from a fight in self-defense, supported by a clear majority of the people, against a limitless rising peril, when Hindenburg put an end to their work and entrusted the helm of state to an adventurous intriguer. Hindenburg was also reproached for having shown the deepest ingratitude toward Brüning, because Brüning, who clung to him with loyal respect, had just employed all possible government influence in favor of Hindenburg's election as Reich President. Many who voted for Hindenburg were deceived in their expectations and in the sacrifice which they had made; for the Social Democratic workingmen, who had voted solidly for him, had given a little shock to their hearts in entrusting themselves to the Prussian field marshal. On the other hand, since the workingmen's vote for him was dictated by a higher and purer necessity, their general attitude, if it had remained unyielding, would have justified Hindenburg's ingratitude toward them and Brüning.

What a lamentable impression, however, is made by the influences that were then pressing in upon the weak old man! First of all was the illusion about the value of the Hitler movement for the German nation and the blindness to the criminal elements in it, which might easily have been discerned by anyone who had eyes. Then there were those sentiments and hopes of the Reichswehr, of which we have already heard, which embodied persistent Prussian influences of Frederick the Great's time although narrowed in spirit and outlook as a result of holding office. A very sad impression is made by two other motives which Hindenburg appears to have produced as the reasons for his dissatisfaction with Brüning's conduct of office. What follows was told me at the time by a trustworthy person. At the last or next to last time that Brüning was received by Hindenburg, he first requested from the Reich President an extension of his authority so that he could proceed more energetically. Thereupon Hindenburg read from a previously prepared piece of paper the following counter-requests: (1) that in the future the government should in general be oriented to the right; (2) that there should be an end to the trade-union secretaries' economic program; (3) that there should be an end to "agrarian bolshevism." Point 2 meant a break with the Social Democratic workingmen — with precisely that social class which had conducted the most determined fight against Hitler and in favor of the Weimar Constitution. Point 3 dealt with the draft of a law for dividing up the Junker estates in East Prussia which seemed to be beyond further rescue because of their excessive indebtedness. This proposal worried the East Prussian estate owners in Hindenburg's neighborhood. For our historical information it is urgently to be desired that these neighborhood influences and the persons responsible for them should be brought into the clearest light. I myself ought not to pass over these things wholly in silence, because they were discussed in serious circles at the time and in still more detail than I should dare to give here. Hindenburg's upright character is not supposed to be doubted in this matter. But the atmosphere around him was thick and murky, and his own capacity for making political judgments was not large.

In this matter of his capacity for making judgments all of us who had cast our ballots with full confidence for Hindenburg in the presidential election were deceived. We had interpreted his attitude after the collapse of 1918, when he offered his hand to Ebert, and his hitherto constitutionally

correct conduct in office since 1925 as signs of a freer, statesmanlike, self-conquering attitude of mind. Today the question is whether this attitude cannot be explained more simply by a trait in character said to have been described by
himself — "to allow one's self to be shoved with dignity."

His decisions to dismiss Brüning and to summon Hitler
stand in the very forefront of the factors leading Germany
along the path to the abyss. The chance trait in Hindenburg's
personality stands therefore at the very center of the general
causes that drove Germany forward on this path, like a dark
warning sign to the final insoluble riddles of world history.

9 THE POSITIVE ELEMENTS IN HITLERISM

It was my opinion at the time and still is that the German
people could have very well been able, under the leadership
of a man like Brüning, to survive the existing conditions and
spiritual crisis and to avert the ruinous experiment of the
Third Reich. Brüning's downfall was brought about by the
closely associated interests of militarists, big industrialists,
and large landed-estate owners. The historical question now
arises, however, whether this Hitler experiment was really, as
its lamentable outcome seems to indicate, ruinous in all its
aspects. Was it not after all borne along by a higher historical
necessity, which must certainly be called tragic because it
ended in disaster, but which, nevertheless, contributed perhaps fruitful ideas that were more than mere weapons in the
battle for power? If so, such ideas, even after the downfall of
those who held them, might retain some value, whether by
perpetuating the memory of a gigantic heroic resolve, or by
their own practical survival in new forms of effort.

This question, whether Hitler's thousand-year Reich contained valuable and viable elements, not for a thousand years,
to be sure, as he imagined, but just perhaps for our own century, occupied many persons otherwise opposed to him during

the twelve years of oppression. The many fortune-seeking opportunists who supported him were very zealous in giving an affirmative answer to this question. But it is also a political and historical duty of conscience to pass judgment on one's own self and on one's own former ideals and to test as far as possible without prejudice the new ideals that were offered to us Germans. The underlying Satanism that rose to heights along with the ideals certainly ought never to be forgotten. But what great, new, existence-changing idea is there in which Satan has not insinuated himself both as driver and as beneficiary! How horrible to us seems the attempt made once before in Germany to found a thousand-year reign, the reign of the Anabaptists in Münster in 1535. Yet that Anabaptist movement in general contained seeds of great fruitfulness for religion and for ways of looking at the world.

We recall what we said at the beginning: the pressure exerted on all existence by the increased masses of population; arising from this pressure, the two waves, nationalist and socialist, of the nineteenth and twentieth centuries; the way the waves criss-crossed and worked upon each other and finally strove to unite. If this union had succeeded, new and unsuspected forms of life might have grown out of them. Friedrich Naumann's proposals, rich in ideas, were an initial theoretical attempt in the direction of this union. They failed because the ideal prerequisites broke down before the coarser mentality and the selfish egotistical group-interests of the conflicting political parties and social groups. But Naumann's attempt survived nevertheless in the work of the Weimar Republic, to which Naumann always remained true and to which he devoted his last strength. His idea survived, to be sure only in a weakened form, moderately and without brilliance, in the necessary Weimar Constitution, over which lay the heavy weight of the Versailles Treaty. Added to all this was the depressing picture of a parliamentary system gone to seed and choked with weeds; the quarrels of lesser officials at the formation of every new cabinet; and finally the scandals of corruption which certainly were immeasurably exaggerated by the Hitler propaganda. Brüning was undoubtedly on the way toward creating a firm governmental authority at the center of the state by strengthening the presidential power. But whatever success he had in this contributed only to his own downfall. Hindenburg would scarcely have dared in the earlier years to have dismissed a chancellor who was opposed by no parliamentary majority. Hitler, however, apparently offered much stronger remedies for all the ills and needs of the time. And the big idea that was floating in the air — the idea of the amalgamation of the nationalist and socialist movements — unquestionably found in him the most ardent spokesman and the most determined practitioner. His share in this great objective idea must be fully recognized.

Hitler wanted to overtrump the bourgeois, class-egotistical nationalism of his heavy-industry patrons and money providers, and also the Marxism of the Russian bolshevists, which he attacked with special zeal and which wanted to condemn the bourgeoisie to extinction. He therefore seized upon the idea that the creation of a new fruitful folk community need not rest upon the one-sided victory of the one or the other of the social forces contending against one another — that the natural groupings of society did not have to be unceremoniously destroyed — but that they must be steered around and educated to serve a community which included them all. Hitler's undertaking seemed to promise more continuity with the traditions and values of the existing bourgeois culture than the radical new edifice of bolshevism. With this idea he bribed a wide circle of citizens. The working class, he intended, should be inspired with the full pride that their productive work merited and thereby lose all their inferiority complexes which sprang from the beginnings of the class struggle. The same fundamental idea of nurturing the special pride of the professional classes and amalgamating them with the all-embracing community was also extended to the peasantry. There was no lack of specious enticements for all classes — celebrations, festivals, and so forth.

The liberal era of the nineteenth century, however imperishable its service in awakening the powers of the individual, had left society too much to itself and allowed the old ethical ties such as family, custom, and social stratification to relax while no energetic consideration was given to the creation of new ties. Society was in danger of becoming amorphous. Already young people were growing up more or less neglected, and the abolition of military service after the Versailles Treaty lessened the educational influence of the state upon the coming generation. Here also the new Hitler state took hold with firm hands and created, even prior to the reintroduction of universal military service, those youth organizations which were expected to give the whole coming generation uniform basic conceptions and at the same time to satisfy the natural impulses of youth.

Romanticism and technology likewise were brought into play in all these new articulations. In technology everything was reckoned out and measured off with a view to forcing it into the service of the new state and to suppressing any divergent individual movement. Men were handled as though they were thoroughly plastic material, like sand and gravel pressed into cement building blocks. This means that the romanticism used for this purpose was not genuine, because genuine romanticism is by nature irrational. It recognizes and desires, to be sure, the articulation of the individual through a community spirit and folk spirit, but always through the irrational spiritual forces of feeling and phantasy and through a certain amount of individual movement. It sounded perhaps romantic enough when we Germans were told to nurture old usages and customs and to go in suddenly for high-pressure genealogical researches concerning our families and ancestors. But the ancestor certificate received in return was simply a well-calculated device for carrying on the fight against the Jews, for the civil degrading of the German-Jewish "hybrids," and for preserving the purity of the Nordic race. But how this Nordic race could then be forgotten and sacrificed, whenever the fight for power in the world was at stake, we have already seen in the case of the alliance that Hitler signed with Japan.

Within the Nordic race, our own German nation was further especially hallowed and in appearance romanticized by the German idea of a people distinguished from other peoples by possessing certain common customs, traditions and historic past, that is, by the idea of a "folk" (*Volk*). In the folk idea, if anywhere, one might be inclined to credit the Nazis with a genuine though immeasurably inflated romantic folk feeling. But one would be disillusioned if one heard of a Nazi practice that was employed in the Warthe district of West Prussia where those Poles who might figure as Germans by reason of their appearance and attitude were absorbed into the German folk-community after an appropriate schooling and probationary period. Himmler even had racially usable elements of the Russian people brought to Germany and educated and drilled as Germans. One is reminded here of the old Turkish institution, the Janizaries. Looked at from the standpoint of naked, heartless power politics, the procedure was certainly not an unpractical one.

One can imagine that the folk idea might survive Hitler's downfall. Here we must distinguish between the two different sides of what people are accustomed to call folk character. There is a peaceful folk character and a fighting folk character — a folk character of purely inner culture and a folk character of political calculation, whether for defensive self-preservation or for offensive extension of power; a kind of German-internal folk character and a borderland folk character; a folk character of genuine romanticism and a folk character in which romanticism is a weapon for conflict, and therefore easily a means to an end and easily spurious, just as we have seen that it was in the case of Hitlerism. The peaceful, cultural German-internal folk character was first taught by Herder and was exemplified for us in a wonderfully poetic manner and with a most genuine romanticism by Jakob Grimm. It is to be hoped that it will continue to live in us Germans to bless us, but it was not bestowed on us by Hitler. The borderland, fighting form of folk character that Hitler represented is not even specifically German, but is a common character of all the nationalities living in the middle ground of eastern Europe and treading on each other's toes. Every oppressed nationality there will defend itself with complete justice and will regard as holy its fight for self-preservation. But as regards the methods and consequences of these fights, eastern Europe is markedly different from western Europe — from Switzerland, Belgium, and the relation between Wales and the rest of England. (Ireland perhaps has been an exception.) In eastern Europe these fights are carried on more bitterly and irreconcilably and the result is the Balkanization, the hardening, and the perpetuation of national hatreds, until one side succeeds in completely annihilating its opponents — as threatens us Germans in the East. The horrible expulsion of the German populations from territories that have had a German stamp since the Middle Ages unfortunately does not find us Germans blameless. It is the answer to the fight for the conquest of the East which Hitler undertook to carry on in the grand style and into which he plunged us when he broke loose against Russia in 1941. The borderland folk idea with which he conducted his policy brought us Germans no blessing. It will be remarked that I say nothing at all against the defense of borderland German territory, but rather insist upon it as a holy duty. But the manner in which this fight in the East was carried on became a misfortune for us. Again we recall Grillparzer's saying which was forced from him by what he saw in the East: "Humanity — Nationality — Bestiality."

We were searching for what was "positive" in Hitler's work and found something which corresponded to the objective ideas and needs of our time. One might perhaps add something more, but in doing so one would be only dressing up a little a well-arranged show window that offered the visitor some wares quite good for their price, but with no guarantee that they could really be bought in the store. Inside the store was obscure and in the background yawned a darker abyss into which the innocent purchaser might unexpectedly stumble. Behind every institution praiseworthy in itself in the Third Reich stood the will-to-power of a conditioned organization — gigantic in extent and soulless in content — the counterpart of which one might find among the Jacobins of 1793 or among the conquering Mongol princes of the Middle Ages. Every fanaticism dries up the soul, and "fanatic" was Hitler's pet word for all his pressure methods. This fanaticism was dedicated to power for its own sake, and all ideas or what passed for ideas were ingeniously used as a means to an end. But power for its own sake means nothing more than placing one's own self at the center of all life. With Hitler this ended in the cult of himself, in the exaggerated belief in his mission by means of what, in his very egocentric feeling, he called "Providence." Here one can constantly recognize a covering wrapper for what might be called his awareness of an ability to prophesy. "I am indeed only a statesman," Mussolini is reported to have said to Hitler at their first meeting in Venice in the spring of 1934, "but you are also a prophet." If one reads the short characterization which Jakob Burckhardt gives in his lectures on Mohammed, one can apply them almost word for word to Hitler. This prophetic element in him, however, must not be rated too highly, for he had no real religion to proclaim in his racial mania but only a very effective means to power, which he could lay aside wherever it did not fit. More likely the roots of his belief in his mission are to be sought in the resentment of the frustrated artist. He had failed to become famous as a painter. But he became aware of his power of working upon his fellowmen through words, through his fiery speeches, when he came to the spiritually crushed men in Munich after the First World War. A Munich professor who was then giving a course for war veterans is said to have been impressed by one soldier among them who talked, talked, talked. That was Hitler.

There was too much ego in Hitler's nature for him to be regarded as a man of superior rank in history. The boundless vanity, the bad taste of his self-glorification, and the senseless robber regime for which he exploited his people's last bit of strength as he clung to the remnants of his power — all these were heavy mortgages which lay on his resolves. Napoleon I, with whom Hitler may in many respects be compared, also had quite ordinary and egocentric traits. But his share in the objective ideas of his time was greater than that which we are able to recognize in Hitler. Napoleon was more rational as a ruler and left behind him positive creations which have proved their value in history. Hitler, however, has left us only a complete heap of ruins.

10 HITLERISM AND BOLSHEVISM

However, it may be objected even by men who were themselves critically inclined against Hitler: Was there not after all a quite positive element in what Hitler wanted to do — in his fight against bolshevism and in his aim of protecting Germany and Europe from it? Even if Hitler failed in these aims, has not failure been the fate of many a historic personality whose great resolve, ending tragically, must nevertheless excite us?

It is not possible here and now to answer exhaustively these questions, which I myself hold to be doubtful and distorted. We know too little of present-day Russia to gauge the extent of the danger which may have threatened us. Did she have the idea of a revolutionary world conquest? Or had her aims changed? Had bolshevism to a certain extent become nationalized and concentrated on the task of consolidating the giant country and raising the land and people to a higher economic level? Today we can express only surmises about these fundamental questions. The reports and impressions that we get from our German war veterans or from Russian prisoners are contradictory. But one thing we can nevertheless gather with certainty from them is the knowledge that terror alone could not have forged the tremendous defensive and offensive power of the Russian masses in their fight against us Germans. From a reliable source we heard the following summary of ever-repeated statements by Russian war prisoners: "We all feel that we are brothers. We have no exploiting class over us. We all work for one another. We die gladly for our country." Are these mere words that were drilled in and repeated for the occasion? One cannot escape the impression that the Russian people opposed us with much greater inner cohesion and national consciousness than in Tsarist days. The thin bourgeois class that formerly existed there is, to be sure, destroyed, but the intellectual level of the masses has risen. Technology and the natural sciences are zealously and successfully cultivated. All the qualms that we had, from the standpoint of the German idealistic and liberal view of life, about the complete imposition of the Russian system upon Germany certainly continue to exist. But the same fundamental rights, which we claim for ourselves, of self-determination and of forming our existence according to our very own folk spirit, we must also concede to the Russians.

Hitler thought otherwise. He had made, so it was said here and there among us, the gigantic attempt to preserve Germany from a monstrous future danger. To this it must immediately be replied that he made it with a gigantic dilettantism. In eight weeks he hoped by a lightning war to strike down the far-flung giant country just as he had succeeded in striking down France in 1940. But he knew little about Russia's deep interior and hidden resources. (The Norwegian Quisling, who played himself up as a strategist and expert on Russia, is said to have especially advised Hitler on this subject.) Moreover this campaign against Russia was attempted at a time when the war against another world power was still undecided and when the third great world power was already standing threateningly in the background and supporting England's fight. Napoleon's undertaking in 1812, under the simpler conditions of those days, had a distinctly more rational character than the Hitler undertaking of 1941, which was claimed to be technically prepared. It was one of those momentous errors in calculation that a technically trained and phantasy-swollen mentality can easily commit nowadays. It reminds one of the Schlieffen plan of campaign. In both cases *homo faber* overreached himself, but Hitler's false cal-

culation was to turn out much more disastrously than Schlieffen's.

Further criticisms can be made. Did Hitler himself, as he so
often proclaimed, regard the defense against bolshevism as the
central point of his policy and strategy? His agreement with
Russia in August 1939, which at once opened to her a wide
path of advance to the West — to Finland, the Baltic provinces, and eastern Poland — tells a different story. One might
perhaps attempt to justify it as *Realpolitik,* as a "shifty" ac-
commodation to gain time for crushing Poland and the Western powers, and then have a final reckoning with Russia
afterwards. It may be so. But one can also attribute to the
"shifty" man the further idea of forming a partnership with
Russia for joint rule over the world — just until the time
should come to expel the Russian partner from the business
and crush him. The fate of the populations in the Baltic
provinces remained a secondary consideration with Hitler.

That it was Hitler's final purpose to crush Russia some
time or other cannot be doubted. His program for it in *Mein
Kampf* is well known. He now departed from his earlier program — to his undoing — only in so far as he originally
planned to wage war against Russia with his rear free toward
the West, in fact in alliance with England if possible — while
in 1941 he repeated the fundamental mistake of the First
World War in having Germany's armies tied down against
both Russia and England at the same time. But the aim of the
offensive war suddenly launched against Russia in 1941 was
the same as that announced in *Mein Kampf*: to make Russia
a German colony and exploit her as a future German place of
settlement. The crusade against bolshevism, however, which
he proclaimed, formed, we are convinced, merely a façade for
this conquest and exploitation. Prior to the year of the outbreak of war in 1939 the audience at one of the training
schools at Tölz was given a revelation about this Nazi policy.
The lecturer was talking about Darré's law for hereditary
homesteads. "It is much criticized today," he said, "and in
view of the situation at present indeed justly criticized. But

just get clear in your minds that it is intended for a wholly different situation. Just think of England. Three hundred years ago she was an island; today she is a world empire. Nowadays things move faster. Just think of a German Reich extending to the Urals — and then the effect of the hereditary homestead law." My informant, who was a wag, asked the lecturer whether Siberia, beyond the Urals, was not also a fine land. "Certainly," was the answer, "we can get Siberia, too, for ourselves."

Hitler's preaching against bolshevism, therefore, was a mask for his will to conquer. That does not exclude the fact that he also worked himself up subjectively into a hatred of bolshevism. But the stronger psychological force in him was the urge for power, the will to conquer. And in the end his conduct in the final desperate struggle indicates that he did not feel too deeply about preserving Germany from bolshevism. The future history of the world may perhaps depend on which of the steadily advancing enemies should have reached Berlin first, the Anglo-Saxons or the Russians. From the moment that the defensive war against both West and East proved hopeless, an absolute opponent of bolshevism would have tried to stop the flood of the Russian attack, as long as was any way possible, in order to give the Anglo-Saxons the chance to get to Berlin first. But Hitler, when he was told of the giant preparations of the Russians for their last great offensive beginning in January 1945, is said to have declared the Russian danger to be of "secondary importance." At any rate, he had already acted as though it was when he precipitated the Christmas offensive against the West on the Belgian front. It gained him nothing except ephemeral prestige, and it withdrew most valuable forces from the defensive campaign in the East. Then in western Germany east of the Rhine, he allowed a bitter fight to continue while the Russian waves of attack were already beginning to threaten Berlin. So one is forced to the surmise that in his desperate mood he either consciously or unconsciously preferred to see the Russians rather than the Anglo-Saxons in Berlin. In other words, at the end, in spite of the sympathy for English world power which he often proclaimed but which was merely calculated opportunism, western democracy was still more hated by him than was bolshevism.

One more Hitler remark made during the war years, which bears on this discussion, may be repeated here, with the reservation that I consider it only inherently probable but not completely authenticated. It comes, I surmise, from the circle around Admiral Raeder. A little pamphlet was laid before Hitler that was intended for distribution in the army as a reminder to the soldiers of the German faith in God in their fight against bolshevism. "God? Religion?" Hitler is reported to have said. "Terror is the best God. One sees that in the case of the Russians. Otherwise they wouldn't fight so."

11 HITLERISM AND CHRISTIANITY

We come now to the subject of Hitlerism and Christianity. Both Marxism and Hitlerism reject Christianity and seek to replace it by a new belief in a coming earthly happiness. Marxism, however, does this openly and resolutely, while Hitler's National Socialism prior to his seizure of power made the pretense, as his program expressed it, that he stood "on the ground of positive Christianity." Then when he came to power, he began to restrict more and more the sphere of action of the Christian church, at first cautiously and privily, in his training courses for Nazis as well as by numerous little administrative measures, by various strokes of the paw against courageous clergymen, by the transformation of some of the old cathedrals into National Socialist monuments, and so forth. In this way he intended, one suspects, to prepare men for the day when the new Hitler religion would be proclaimed and the new faith, long and repeatedly resounding in the Führer's speeches, would receive its highest consecration. Did he not perhaps intend some day, as was whispered in party circles, to organize after the final victory a celebration of this kind at Marienburg? Meanwhile, Hitler believed that he must continue to make use of "the Lord God" and "Providence" for propaganda purposes on suitable occasions, and to dangle them on the stage by a string in order to satisfy his hearers who were accustomed to fine Christian phrases.

What was it that fundamentally distinguished Hitler and Christianity from one another? Christianity, or rather men who gave themselves out to be Christians, had been able in the course of history to adapt themselves to the most varied political attitudes and had even bestowed the blessing of the church on the most dubious political systems. An attempt of this kind, to put on the stage a "German Christianity" and to create for it a "Reich Bishop" was actually made, with the Protestant church as a basis. But it failed very lamentably because of the spiritual inadequacy of the personnel available for it. Hitler himself dropped the bishop without giving a word of public explanation. The whole idea might be attributed to his boundless impulse toward self-importance and to the desire to crown his role as prophet by becoming the founder of a new religion. What he understood by "religion" he is said to have put on paper in a little pamphlet which was later carefully suppressed. It corresponded fairly closely, I was told, with what one can read in Rosenberg's *Der Mythus des 20. Jahrhunderts.* Nietzsche's well-known indictment against the slave morality of Christianity was probably reflected in the master religion of the Nordic race which was to be proclaimed by Hitler.

Hitler's deepest hatred of Christianity, however, was directed, it seems to us, toward something else: the idea inherent in Christianity of an independent conscience answerable only to God; the command to obey God rather than man and to recognize a Kingdom that is not of this world and to obey laws other than those proclaimed by National Socialism. All these things brought Hitler to the correct recognition of the fact that here was a deep source of resistance against the totalitarian uniform leveling of inward and outward life. As to the dogmas of Christianity, he never once wanted to quarrel with Pastor Niemöller. These, in his opinion, could continue to be quietly proclaimed without injury to himself. But the right to an independent religious examination of one's own conscience he could not pardon in the brave pastor and former submarine captain.

Niemöller himself had at first placed hopes in Hitler. But as soon as the un-Christian and anti-Christian trait in Hitler's purposes broke forth, Niemöller's duty to his own conscience broke through his former illusions and he became the preacher of protest, to whose pulpit in Dahlem men from all Berlin crowded. Because of this Hitler let him sit in the Dachau concentration camp from the autumn of 1937 until the end of the war.

Niemöller, however, represented without knowing it much more than the mere doctrines of his church. The whole past of Christian Western culture of two millenniums rose up in him and called to the usurper of that past: "My kingdom, saith the Lord, is not of this world, but thy kingdom, that thou wouldst establish, is of Satan."

One must comprehend in quite a wide sense the character of this Christian past which rebelled against Hitler. Liberalism and democracy, both things that Hitler ardently hated, also belonged, rightly understood, to this past and had been able to develop historically only on the basis of Christianity, through a graded series of modifications and secularizations. The French Declaration of the Rights of Man and of the Citizen of 1789, as writers have shown, had Christian religious roots in the basic right of freedom of conscience on which the democratic Puritans of Rhode Island had founded their constitution. Inside the Christian Western world there had been plenty of hatred and fights between positive conscientious Christianity on the one side and modifications and secularizations on the other. How deep appeared the abyss between the humanitarian Freemasons and the Catholic church! Yet now these seeming archenemies all at once joined hands in the same defensive fight against the rise of a new heathenism and — one may now venture to say so — were thereby fighting against a new but wholly different kind of secularization. For the last tie was severed which connected previous secularizations with dogmatic Christianity: recognition of the human conscience as the proclaimer of divine and eternal commandments, above all of the moral commandment to love one's neighbor as one's self. This moral law implies the recognition of human dignity in everyone we meet, even though he belong to a wholly foreign race; it means moral restraints even in wars of peoples and nations! In historical practice, to be sure, these moral restraints had been trampled upon often enough by those whom we regard, in a narrower or wider sense, as offshoots of the Christian civilization of the West. But the spur of conscience always remained active in the nations, and excesses were usually followed by a recalling of the basic moral commandments. People did not dare to set them aside completely.

Hitler and his followers dared to do so, perhaps not all along the line because that would have led to anarchy and chaos. In the *Volkswohlfahrt* (People's Welfare), which was based on something resembling love-thy-neighbor ethics, much was done, and in part not ineffectively. But national egoism limited this welfare work fundamentally to the German people, and within the German people only to those groups which did not oppose National Socialist leadership and did not seem politically dangerous. With regard to all others, especially the hated Jews, there were no longer any moral restraints or a recognition of the rights of man and of human dignity. This was not said openly, and for tactical reasons a different tone might now and then be sounded. But in the gas chambers of the concentration camps the last breath of the Christian feeling for humanity and of the Christian culture of the West was finally extinguished.

The new edifice of the Third Reich began with the oppression of conscience by a terrorism that flooded in through countless channels or gently and unceasingly infiltrated the life of every single individual in the nation. In this oppression we see the strongest and most poisonous of the Nazi measures and the Nazi's own original sin. This more frivolous oppression of conscience was different in nature from that which any religion or public opinion seeking domination had ever been able to exercise. Religions which aim at domination exercise oppression not merely from a desire for domination but also, one might say, from an exaggerated duty of conscience and a zeal for the salvation of the soul — that is, from spiritual narrowness of mind. Public opinion also is restrained when it exercises oppression and is also usually accompanied by a quasi-ethical conviction that a decent person must think thus and so, and not otherwise. But the oppression of conscience exercised on the people after the Nazi party had gained domination resulted quite predominantly from the lack of conscience in those who exercised the oppression. It was used unscrupulously as an agency of power to nip in the bud every kind of popular resistance against the pressure of the party.

The following instance is the most important example of this unscrupulous oppression. The party notoriously had no popular majority behind it when it came to power, as the election figures cited above show. Furthermore, in the Reichstag which was elected under pressure and terror in the spring of 1933, the Nazis even by reckoning for themselves the German Nationalists led by Hugenberg still were not able to gather the two-thirds majority necessary for changes in the constitution. Therefore, the Enabling Act (by which the constitution was changed, by which Hitler became all-powerful, by which also he was put into a position to do the greatest harm) could be passed only with the voting support of parties which opposed the Hitler regime. This voting support was actually obtained. The Catholic Center and the few Democrats in the Reichstag voted on March 23, 1933, for the Enabling Act which was especially hateful to them. The fear that terrorism would mount still further had enfeebled in them the voice of political conscience. The day before the vote was taken, I asked a Center deputy with whom I was acquainted: "You will certainly vote against it?" He shrugged his shoulders and replied: "Then things would get even worse."

The evil went further. Action or consent of this kind, resulting from fear and condemned by one's own conscience, demoralizes a people, and did, in no small degree, demoralize us Germans. An old friend said to me in the early years, gnashing his teeth: "One half of the German people today are educated to insolence and the other half to cowardice." This means that in those who unscrupulously exercised this oppression of conscience, their own consciences withered away — the last moral tie, the remnant of the Christian spirit, ceased to exist. The Third Reich was not only the greatest misfortune that the German people have suffered in their existence, it was also their greatest shame.

12 HITLERISM AND THE WESTERN POWERS

In the camp of the Western powers the danger which threatened the world from National Socialism was regarded as greater and at any rate more pressing than that which was to be feared from Russian bolshevism. They much preferred to unite with the latter to crush Hitlerite Germany. By their common victory, for which Russia had to do most, they opened a broad opportunity to her for the future. This result was possible only because of the rise of Hitler and the Third Reich. We shall not inquire what kind of a world situation might have developed without him. We shall inquire here only into the motives which can have given the Western powers the greater fear of Hitlerism.

Without question the motives were first and foremost those of power politics. The Hitler danger was immediate and acute. Unless it was combated, all Europe would be turned into a Hitler-German sphere of power, not of course all at once, but step by step. People knew from the First World War what Germany was able to accomplish with her concentrated potential in men and material resources. The explosive forces gathered by Hitler pressed for a quicker, and at the moment a more dangerous, outlet than those being assembled in Russia in slower economic constructive work. The Western powers after all might perhaps have regarded Russia with the expectation that she would renounce the idea of world revolution, confine herself to constructive work at home, and draw closer to democratic ideas. Who would want to deny that behind all considerations of power politics on the part of the Western powers there existed a general distrust of Germany? As a German, I deplore it, suffer under it, and feel myself compelled to inquire about the deeper causes of this distrust.

Behind the growing pressure of increased masses of population and behind all the power politics and wars of states since the French Revolution stands the struggle for the way of life of the individual nations. By way of life we mean here the totality of the mental and material habits of life, the institutions, customs, and way of thinking. All of these seem to be bound together by an inner tie, by some guiding principle from within, to form a large, not always clearly definable but intuitively understandable, unity. In the great European wars the aristocratic way of life of the *ancien régime* was the first to be destroyed. Today the democratic-bourgeois way of life, especially as it has developed in the Western world, is threatened. To this way of life belongs not only the rule of the majority in the state and along with it a growing pressure of the masses and a certain leveling of social classes, but also a restriction of this leveling process as a result of the freer play of economic forces — by capitalism which enables the individual equipped for it to become rich and powerful. The moral and spiritual life, the culture of nations as well as of individuals, can both suffer severely from the leveling process and recover again in the surging up and down of these economic forces. General criticisms of this democratic way of life, whether to glorify it or to condemn it, have no place here. But whoever regards the inner moral self-determination of man and with it his freedom of conscience and freedom of thought as the first conditions of all higher and true culture — such a person must, even if with some resignation, admit that it is altogether possible to prepare a place for the spirit and for culture in Western democracy. The actual tyranny of the complex of economic power and of social convention can easily narrow the spirit and culture seriously. But there has not yet disappeared in the ideology of nations the old hard-won fundamental right of the Christian Western world, the right to freedom of conscience and of thought. There still rings in the ears of the writer of these lines the words which he heard from the lips of President Franklin Roosevelt in 1936 at the three-hundredth anniversary celebration of Harvard University: "In this day of modern witch-burning, when *freedom of thought* has been exiled from many lands which were once its home, it is the part of Harvard and America to stand for the freedom of the human mind and to carry the torch of truth." The robbing us Germans of our freedom of thought, which is imputed to the Third Reich, constitutes perhaps if not the most effective at least the most essential reason for the deep aversion of the Western nations toward Hitler's Germany.

Roosevelt's words point at the same time to the deep chasm which exists between Hitler's Germany and the former Germany in which we grew to greatness. In the Bismarckian Reich, as in the Weimar Republic, we still enjoyed a sufficient measure of freedom of conscience and thought. Granted, the authoritarian and militarist element that also contributed to our way of life in the Bismarckian Reich accustomed many persons to subordinate their way of thinking to the wishes of their superiors and made them spiritually dependent. But this element had at that time not yet become a mortal danger. The syntheses of classical liberalism, which sought to bring spirit and power into harmony, had not yet died out. They even experienced around the turn of the century a certain revival in a new form, and many good seeds sprouted and blossomed in the years before August 1914. To be sure, the weeds of striving for power and pleasure also sprouted and luxuriated, but the inner bond between the German way of life and the Western way of life had not yet been severed. There was still a common Occidental Christian atmosphere — using here the word "Christian" in its widest sense of regard for freedom of conscience. Then the First World War seemed to destroy the bond. We were reproached by the West with having deserted the old, better German spirit, which was also the Occidental spirit, and were charged in general with the cult of brute force. We denied this with a clear conscience — but already in the course of the World War we ourselves had to realize that there was something to the charges, however extreme they were. A new German way of life grew ominously strong and allowed man's conscience to remain silent where questions concerning the acquisition of national power were involved. This trend later increased as a result of the effects of the Versailles Treaty. We have noted above how these effects influenced the old way of life during the Weimar Republic and have showed how the republic suffered under them. A new German way of life reached extreme forms in the Hitler movement, in the radical breaking away from all moral restraints in the struggle for power, and in a way of life devoid of conscience.

The western part of the Occident looked at this development with interest and distrust, but without a clear understanding of what was at stake for the whole West if Hitler should triumph and if the effort of the Weimar system to keep the German way of life in harmony with that of the West should fail. The peoples of the West felt themselves all too safe in their own mighty strength and spheres of power, which they enjoyed as a heaven-sent and well-earned blessing. They were not in the least worried about maintaining their own way of life. They could calmly let the experiment of Fascism go on before their eyes, because if it led to war it must fail because of Italy's weakness. Moreover, Mussolini had declared that his Fascism was a national Italian affair and not an article for export, not merely because of his propagandist calculation but also because he really meant what he said. England's own little fascist movement, which was connected with the name of Mosley, was not taken very seriously.

But now with Hitler came something new, not indeed absolutely new, but new in its consequences and its possibilities for the future. A fascism had already sprung up from minorities which were very small at first, but were resolute and unscrupulous. It gathered bold, insolent fellows who were attracted to it by their purely personal itch for power and for making themselves important. Nationalist ideology, however, was the main thing with them. We have already noted in connection with the Hitler movement that the inner genuineness of this ideology was pretty dubious — that it could be forgotten or laid aside whenever naked power-interests so demanded. That, of course, was never to be divulged or admitted to the great mass of faithful followers. It remained the secret of internal, very small, circles of the Leadership Elite. Into this, however, a sharp observer like Rauschning in his *Revolution of Nihilism* was early able to penetrate. The NSDAP (*Nationalsozialistische Deutsche Arbeiter-Partei*) was an eminently hierarchical organization which transformed ordinary nonpolitical associations into regular Nazi party organizations, like the National Socialist Women's Organization, the National Socialist Teachers' Union, and so forth. These were pressed together by a compelling fear for their own existence. These organizations were again divided and subdivided into ever smaller circles. But at their top stood persons who were ready for any infamous action — criminal natures, Catilines — not all pure criminals, but combinations of rascality and stupidity, as we observed earlier, in whom a brutalized phantasy might give to their own criminal actions the consecration of a higher mission, even a universal mission for a reforming of the whole world according to the Hitler model. The phrase "world planning" arose among these circles.

And this phantasy was not wholly without a real foundation. In every land, in every nation, there was a small fringe of persons who were both rascals and fools, with whom one could come into contact and who could be animated by the successful example of the Hitler movement to undertake the same thing in their own country. We saw this in Quisling in Norway, in Mussert in the Netherlands, in the Nazi mouthpieces in Switzerland, and in the states of southeastern Europe. Everywhere such fringes of Little Hitlers were immediately at hand and went to work. The Foreign Section (*Auslandsorganisation*) of the NSDAP then tried to bring together such fringes — "cells" they were called — in America, primarily in South America (Argentina) and apparently also in the United States. The Hitler movement thus acquired a universal character. A new International was arising with the purpose of driving out of the field in course of time the other existing Internationals (communists, Roman Catholics, banking groups, and so forth). It might have sounded as its slogan: "Catilines of all countries, unite!"

Now for the first time perhaps we understand fully why the Western Nations were determined to do their uttermost to combat the Hitler danger. To the motives of power politics which we have noted, to the uneasiness which Germany's authoritarian and militarist structure at the time of the Bismarckian Reich had already caused them, there was now added a new danger. This danger was that this new Germany, since it had also increased the authoritarian militarism to an unheard-of maximum, might cause annoyance to them in their own land by an international propaganda; might stir up revolution; and in the end, if this succeeded, might even rob them of their existing way of life. It might perhaps be like that plague several centuries ago when a few germs brought from overseas sufficed to fill all the streams with their rank growth.

Against bolshevism the Western nations believed themselves to be immune. Fascism renounced all intention of being an export article. Hitlerism, on the other hand, suddenly brought forward in the world market a new export article which had refined techniques that were quickly adaptable to every country. The raw material of this article consisted to a certain degree of racial ideology with its central point of hatred against the Jews. Of this there was already a certain amount in every country, or it could be stimulated. But the refining of this raw material took place in the Nazi hierarchical organization. It aimed at winning the masses and satisfying their instinct for quasi-ideas; it stirred up everywhere the ambition of men to become little *Führers* and offered the highest enjoyment of power and every desired benefit as the privilege of a small elite of human beasts of prey. When the racial ideology and hatred of the Jews was somewhat ineffective as raw material for the needs of the masses, some other ideology, hatched by theorists or sects, could be substituted for it and duly pumped up. Ideologies no longer sit so very securely at the stage where a culture has shallowed out into a civilization. They are not everywhere genuine. They can under circumstances be easily exchanged with one another. To recall Goethe's phrase, we do not live in an age of belief, but of unbelief. Beast-of-prey natures, however, are to be found in every age and in every land. They lie hidden in the demonic depths of society, spring forth in times of revolution and unbelief, and then become the *terribles simplificateurs* whom Jakob Burckhardt saw were arising in the Occident.

Fears of this kind, we suspect, must have seized upon the souls of the Western nations. The fears did not need to be thought through in all directions. They perhaps did not rise to a clearly formulated conscious expression. And yet they may have caused a gloomy foreboding that the Western democratic and liberal way of life was threatened, thus creating that almost crusading frame of mind with which the war was waged and loosing upon us and our historical monuments the horrible terror from the air.

13 HAS HITLERISM A FUTURE?

The preceding observations raise the fearfully serious question whether Hitlerism, though at present struck down to the ground, may not after all, by the demagogic superiority of its methods of ruling the masses, become the prevailing way of life in the Occident. We have looked for the positive elements in Hitlerism and have found something — the conscious purpose of letting the two waves of the age, the nationalist and the socialist movements, intermingle into one, thereby molding the amorphous classes of society more firmly together within themselves and as a whole. But we have an unconquerable aversion to the methods used in attempting this integration. Men with a Hegelian habit of mind may perhaps overlook these evil methods and content themselves with a philosophy of history that teaches that mankind is accustomed to climb to higher levels only by going through some kind of purgatory — something like the great German migrations long ago. But if this so-called higher level leads to a systematic suppression of conscience — the original source of everything that we regard as divine in and around us — then it would again lead to the abyss. Therefore, so long as conscience is active in mankind and in the individual nations, it will guard itself against this march to the abyss.

A pessimistic philosopher of history, who had learned something from Burckhardt, might nevertheless declare this abyss to be unavoidable. He could point to symptoms of decay in the culture and civilization even of the Western nations and to the way in which the striving of the masses for power and pleasure may some day triumph over nobler motives of an intellectual and ethical sort that still exist. That, of course, is a matter that depends on opinion and not on positive proof. In making such evaluations and drawing the balance between the present moral and the amoral forces of a people, the inborn temperament of the individual, whether inclined to pessimism or optimism, will often play the decisive part. We can, however, perhaps find a more objective way to answer our main question whether defeated Hitlerism can nevertheless be assigned a universal future.

It was certainly a very singular and in no small degree a chance chain of causes which led to Hitler's seizure of power. No pressing necessity of a general sort, as we attempted to show, guided Hindenburg's pen as he signed his name to Hitler's appointment. There were plenty of forces for protection against it. If Hindenburg had let these forces work themselves out, the Hitler movement would presumably have remained only an episode — like that of Thomas Münzer and the kingdom of the Anabaptists at Münster. Its universal future would then have been destroyed.

We are not forgetting, however, that this way of proving the case is not wholly adequate. The first proponents of a new idea, one might object, often are crushed, but the idea triumphs after all through the new proponents that it finds. But was the idea which Hitler represented, one may ask, rich enough in content to inspire new proponents in place of the original proponents who had perished? The following point may be made in answer to this question. What might be regarded as an ideal in Hitler's undertaking is overshadowed by the selfish acquisitive aspect of what was a speculative adventure on the part of a group of reckless gamblers. It might have succeeded through a favorable constellation of circumstances. It might have repeated successes in foreign policy as a result of the known and rightly calculated disinclination of the Western powers for a new war. But these successes were again lost through a frivolous overestimation of this chance luck and an underestimation of the opponents and their potential strength. These are all typical stages in the history of a swindler's venture or of a person playing for high stakes at the gambling table. And the crassly egotistical character of the whole undertaking is then ultimately revealed with frightful clearness in the final collapse. When the Nazis had to recognize that the game was lost and that they themselves were lost, then they intended that the German people should likewise lose and senselessly follow the leaders into the abyss. What was left of the ideal here? To live and die *for* the people, yes, that would have been an ideal. But to sacrifice without conscience the people themselves, that was a fraudulent bankrupt's way of behaving.

There was also too much that was criminal in the doings

and dealings of the Hitler group to make it possible to assign them a higher position in history. However crushing and shameful the fact is that a band of criminals could succeed for twelve years in forcing the German people under its leadership and in bringing a great part of the people to believe that they were following a great ideal — this very fact nevertheless has a calming and comforting aspect. The German people were not fundamentally diseased with criminal sentiments but were only suffering for a while with a severe infection from poison administered to it. If the poison had been allowed to work a long time in the body, then indeed the case might have become hopeless. That was the most troublesome thought that tormented me during the twelve years — that the Nazi party might succeed in maintaining itself at the helm and in stamping upon the whole coming generation its own degenerate character. Outweighing this in my mind, however, was the calculation that the overweening pride of their aims in world politics must bring upon them a frightful end. This of course also turned out to be a frightful end for our whole outward existence and our hard-won national and political gains of earlier times. It was only our inner existence, our souls, our conscience, that could now breathe freely again and give us a span of new life.

Therefore, while I comforted myself with the conviction that the German people would return to their better self after the lesson they had received and would drive out of their blood the parasites of Hitlerism, I never forgot the connections which this Hitlerism had with the whole social and political development that had preceded it: the crazy madness of many of the upper middle class after Bismarck's time, their despiritualization and materialization; the still older narrowing and hardening of the character of Prussian-German militarism; and finally all that was connected with the transformation of *homo sapiens* into *homo faber* and its devastating psychological effects. We have said enough about this already and always come back to the conclusion that all these evil ferments by themselves could not have sufficed to call forth the Hitler spirit. There must therefore have been a special complete break which separates the Hitler movement from all movements of the past and from all that might in any way resemble it in the future. It is one of the great examples of the singular and incalculable power of personality in historical life — in this case of a downright demonic personality. How could any other kind of a personality have been able to organize such a band of criminals as that which fastened upon the German people and sucked them dry? These fellows could have been criminals even without Hitler. But as they came to see him and his magical influence on the masses, they must have said joyfully to themselves: With *him* at our head we can strike; we can conquer all Germany for ourselves. But what kind of a loyalty they must have had to their *Führer* is roughly described in Schiller's *The Robbers*. Look at the case of Röhm, and perhaps also that of Rudolf Hess. And was even Himmler himself loyal to his *Führer* in the last period after July 20, 1944?

Singular therefore was the personality and singular the constellation of circumstances under which alone the party could succeed in coming to power and in compelling the German people for a limited period to follow a false path. This false path led to a region in which a man decent by nature could not long tarry. But from these facts there now arises for the German people the reassuring possibility, as well as the duty, to cleanse themselves of the horror which they have undergone. Let us express our belief about what ought to be considered for this purpose. We want to keep our eye only on what is fundamental and not try to give some kind of formal blueprint for building up Germany again. If we Germans are once agreed among ourselves on fundamentals, if we have made clear our sentiments to one another, then we shall find all the concrete ways and means for their realization. First, however, it is worth while to report on an attempt that was made during the war, but which failed.

14 THE BACKGROUND OF JULY 20, 1944

It would have been a blessing if the German people had found in themselves the strength to throw off the Hitler yoke. But everyone who has lived under the Third Reich knows that it became physically impossible to accomplish this by a general popular movement. "Only by a war shall we be able to get rid of this band of fellows," I once heard murmured by a person who had at first been taken in by them and then been quickly disillusioned. Everything depended upon the attitude of the Reichswehr. It had done its part to help Hitler to power. But among its better and maturer elements might not the illusion about the value of the Hitler movement give way before the recognition of its worthlessness? Might not the Reichswehr some day act in accord with this recognition? That was the sombre hope for the future that many patriots discussed secretly among themselves. This was something tremendous to hope for from the Reichswehr, because their action, from a formal viewpoint, would be nothing less than a military Putsch, something altogether unheard-of in the tradition of the Prussian-Germany army. But also unheard-of was the situation which had been created by Hitler and his party. In a situation of this kind persons who believe that they are standing upon the same ground of moral austerity may all of a sudden feel themselves torn apart. One man is driven by his conscience to condemn any breaking of the military oath sworn to Hitler; another sees it as his higher moral duty to break it in order to free the Fatherland from a gang of criminals and to preserve it from further unforeseeable misfortunes. The ethical problem in Schiller's *Wilhelm Tell* again becomes vital.

The first officer, so far as I know, who had to solve the problem for himself was General von Fritsch, who as Chief of the Army Command had to hand in his resignation at the beginning of 1938 under circumstances which might perhaps have caused him to lead a military uprising against Hitler. But he refrained. Not long afterwards, however, as more harm was done by Hitler, Groener, who was closely associated with General von Fritsch, told me confidentially, as should now be revealed for history: "Fritsch regrets now that he did not act." Then when the war against Poland broke out, Fritsch took part in it as a volunteer without command of troops and died before the enemy's fire before the walls of Warsaw. This account at least seems to me the most probable of the various versions circulating about his death — the death of a soldier with a broken heart.

Then came the icy winter of 1941–42, which almost prepared for us a second 1812 in Russia. Again the question pressed itself to the lips of thoughtful persons: Why do the generals not act? Why do they not atone for the sin they have committed in previously favoring the Hitler movement? Why do they not overthrow the man so dangerous for all? Then I learned toward the end of 1941 that there were generals who had wrestled with themselves and come to see that only by a deed, which from a formal point of view was a crime worthy of death, could Germany be saved from slipping further down toward the abyss. The former Chief of the General Staff, General Beck, who was on the retirement list but who was regarded as one of the ablest heads in the army, said at that time to my informant: "The Gordian knot can be cut only by a single blow of the sword. But the man who deals this blow must know the mighty machine of the German army as well as be master of it."

The action of July 20, 1944, which is connected with the names of Beck and Goerdeler, was therefore already in preparation. My informant was Hermann Kaiser, captain in the Supreme Command in the West. He was a former historian who from now on often sought me out; a glowing idealist, a deeply religious nature, who felt Hitler to be a sin against God, and who worked with determination with Beck and Goerdeler to prepare an uprising out of the center of the armed forces. His first visit to me was concerned with a purely historical question, which, however, was already full of significance for the future. He was making historical researches into the secret political leagues at the time of the War of Liberation, and we discussed the German League of 1812–13 to which Eichhorn and Friesen had belonged. It was linked together through very small groups or "cells," each composed of three or four like-minded companions of whom only one knew anything about the next cell and its confidential member. I remarked that I wondered what he was driving at, and Kaiser then began to disclose Beck's and Goerdeler's plans. The former he referred to by the assumed name Eisenmann, and the latter he similarly called Messer. Then one day he said to me with satisfaction: "Today, among us also, one can regard a German League as in existence." Goerdeler, he reported, had said that he could reckon upon thousands who would help once the main blow had succeeded.

My talks with Kaiser belong to the inwardly most exciting experiences of my life. It was enough for him that I agreed fundamentally with him. Of the preparations in detail I learned but little, and I knew nothing beforehand of the attempt of July 20, 1944. But Kaiser arranged that Beck and I should get in touch with one another and enter into an exchange of views. So I came to be acquainted with one of those unfortunately not too numerous higher officers who can be regarded as the true heirs of Scharnhorst, not only as strict and energetic soldiers, but also as highly cultivated, farseeing patriots.

Beneath Beck's and Goerdeler's plans lay a correct political consideration. The defeat of Germany by the greater potential strength of her opponents, directed by a determined will, was only a question of time, especially after the catastrophe of Stalingrad and the landing of the Americans in Africa. A longer continuance of the Hitler regime could only prolong Germany's agonies, and with a Hitler regime the opponents could never be expected to negotiate. Therefore with Hitler in power nothing was to be expected with certainty except fathomless misfortune. Now if a new government capable of negotiations, supported by an army which, while unable to win would still be able to fight and inspire respect, were to take Hitler's place, then one might hope to obtain more favorable peace terms.

There were many objections, of course, that could be made to these ideas. Undoubtedly, after a successful attempt, a new stab-in-the-back legend was to be expected, a wild cry from the Nazis that the final victory was wrested from Germany by treachery. The Nazis even had the effrontery, only a few weeks before the final catastrophe, to spread the myth of a final victory. Now, whoever placed above everything else the task of preserving Germany from the greatest catastrophe in her history must also have the moral courage to bear the insulting abuse which a second stab-in-the-back legend would heap upon him. Beck and his companions had this courage.

More serious, however, is another objection. Could one be sure that after Hitler's overthrow the army would follow the generals' *Fronde?* Could one be sure that other generals would not oppose their revolt, and that in the face of the enemy a civil war at the front and at home might not flare up? The nazification of the army had already gone a long way when war broke out, and whether the army would recognize Germany's true situation and obey the new government depended not only on the generals, but also on the young lieutenants. The whole undertaking might perhaps fail at the very beginning because of this politically unripe and hitherto sorely misled generation in the officer corps. Whether indeed the attitude of the Berlin Guard Battalion on July 20 was so loyal to Hitler as Goebbels would have us believe is very doubtful according to information that has recently come to me. They are reported to have stood there "neutral" for hours, with stacked arms.

July 20 failed above all else from the chance fact that Hitler remained alive because the explosive bomb, which was calculated for the cement walls of a bunker, did not take full effect in the wooden barracks in which the consultation, quite by exception, took place that day. If Hitler had been killed everything would have depended upon the outcome of the struggle between the new leadership of the army and the

Waffen-SS. The generals would have demanded that the *Waffen*-SS allow itself to be incorporated into the army in order to continue the fight against the foreign enemy, and would only have had to put down by force those parts of the *Waffen*-SS which resisted. But now that Hitler remained alive, the prospects for this plan became much less bright.

In justification of the conspirators, one can also make the point that the misfortunes which would have broken over Germany through a continuance of the Hitler regime seemed to them much greater than the misfortunes of a civil war. The latter, as far as one could see, would be only of short duration, and also the war against the external enemy would then have quickly come to an end. Many cities would have remained undestroyed and many thousand lives would have been saved if the attempt of July 20 had led to some such kind of an outcome — if it had resulted in getting rid of Hitler and in causing a split in the army.

Finally, a last objection can be raised about the manner and the much too long duration of the preparations. More men were drawn into the secret, perhaps had to be drawn in, than was desirable if the secret was to be kept. Incautious things were also done. The long postponement of the undertaking was owing above all else to Beck's severe illness, which led to an operation in 1943. The danger of being betrayed now became continually greater. At the beginning of 1944 Kaiser informed me that the undertaking had in fact been betrayed and must be given up. And when Beck visited me for the last time in the spring of 1944, he said to me: "There is no use. There is no deliverance. We must now drain little by little the bitter cup to the very bitterest end." I surmise now that they finally made the attempt because it had already been betrayed, and because they wanted at least to make a last attempt to save Germany before the threatened mass arrests.

There then occurred, as is well known, a mass execution of those who really were, or were even suspected of being, accomplices. This mass execution was presumably intended to strike down also as many as possible of the men whose task it might be to coöperate in the building up of a new Germany. We Germans were deprived of the services of many valuable and irreplaceable men. It was not at first revealed that among those executed were men like the active Prussian Finance Minister Popitz; the former ambassador in Rome, Ulrich von Hassel; and the former ambassador in Moscow, Count Schulenburg. It was nonsense to speak of the men who carried out the attempt as a reactionary militarist clique. Many names of old familiar families stood beside the names of Social Democrats on the lists which have now been drawn up of those who were executed. These lists apparently include only a small part of those actually put to death. How little of a reactionary Beck himself was, I know from my conversations with him. In my last talk with him in May 1944 he expressed the opinion that after the expected final catastrophe there must be founded an anti-Nazi unity party which would extend from the extreme right to the communists, because, as he had learned in Upper Silesia, the loyalty of the communists in fundamental national questions could be relied upon.

People will probably never reach a unanimous judgment, whether of approval or of condemnation, about the men of July 20. As one who was in the secret in a wider sense, I can only say that I hold their motives to be pure and highminded. They proved to the world that in the German army and in the German people there were still men who were not willing to subject themselves as dumb dogs, but who had the courage for martyrdom.

15 ROADS TO SURVIVAL

So the task of eradicating the poisonous growth of National Socialism passed into the hands of the victors. That made it psychologically difficult for those of us Germans who had privately hoped to accomplish this by our own strength. Many a troubled mind unable to think things through to the end and moved by a feeling of national pride might reject the idea of pulling on the same rope with the former enemies of his country. In fact a quite paradoxical situation arose which was unforeseen in the usual catechism of national duties. In view of all the humiliations now imposed on the whole German people without any exceptions we were expected to place ourselves behind the people and forget all previous strife among ourselves.

But are there not situations in which one must place oneself in front of the people in order to lead them out of illusion into truth? Only he who has made it quite clear to himself that the postwar period of external foreign rule was preceded by a period of inner foreign rule can find the road to a solution of the national problem. External foreign rule is a fearful thing, and for proud peoples deeply humiliating. But the souls of the people do not necessarily and everywhere need to suffer under it. The national feeling of the better people may even in fact be deepened and purified by pain. We know that from our own history. How an inner foreign rule of the kind which was our lot during the Third Reich can work on the soul of the nation and of individuals, we ourselves have only just begun to experience. It clamps upon the soul much more tightly than the external foreign rule, because it is able to work so much more effectively with lies and frauds. It was able to recommend itself by flattering us into thinking that it was the harbinger of great national achievements, like supreme military power and a greater Germany. But even if these aims could have been permanently maintained, they would not have outweighed the sacrifice which a long continuance of the Third Reich would have imposed upon us — the sacrifice of decent sentiments which were so frightfully threatened under this regime. For what is a man profited, if he shall gain the whole world, and lose his own soul?

So far as the victors try to eradicate National Socialist influences and thereby provide the atmosphere for Christian Occidental sound morals, we must not only recognize that they are fundamentally right but must ourselves help them and try to prevent them only from schematic exaggerations and mistakes. The task of eradicating evil dispositions in a people and replacing them by better ones would be insoluble if it was a matter of the great psychological tendencies of the century. Neither the national nor the social ideas of two centuries, nor the desired uniting of them, allowed, or allow, themselves in the long run to be suppressed by force. We shall speak of this later. The hybrid fashion in which Hitler represented both sets of ideas and united them was nothing idealistic but something quite common — it was a criminal purpose. One ought to try to counteract it successfully. That at least is what popular education in all civilized lands has been able to achieve, not absolutely, but to a large degree. The appeal to decent men will find a response in German hearts also. External measures, even those rising to the point of compulsion, are inevitable, as in every kind of popular education. Our foreign masters, as the mighty victors, will apply them plentifully.

Our task then is to give them a real understanding of our conditions. The number of people who compromised with National Socialism — persons without much judgment but at bottom harmless, decent, and even wanting to be idealistic — was enormously large. In their case not only strict justice but also human understanding must be exercised. Not all party members were alike — *distinguendum est* — we cry to our judges, especially we who from the beginning condemned Nazism. It is a matter not only of exercising moderation in individual cases and preserving many private existences from ruin, but also of preventing a general embitterment of the people. Embitterment might spring from a feeling of being treated unjustly, might hinder our inner recovery, and might make Germany into a center of disease of the worst sort. Very great also was the number of those who protested inwardly against Hitler but outwardly yielded for existence's sake. Many who would have mustered up courage for martyrdom for themselves did not do so in order not to plunge their families into misfortune. It was a feature of the Nazi party's refined technique in punishment always to make all one's relatives suffer also.

Now, however, the victors have announced that they intend to eradicate not only National Socialism, but also militarism, as the source of disturbance for the world. Our great power of defense, our system of universal military service, must end. I myself half a century ago had to describe its introduction into Prussia by the Boyen defense law of September 3, 1814, as a great national as well as epoch-making event, and I still stand by this judgment today. But does it not happen in the case of all great and fruitful ideas in world history that in the course of their historical evolution both good and evil can develop out of them? One effect of what we have experienced is that the demonic element hidden in human and historical life rises before our eyes more clearly and disturbingly than previously. So also in the evolution of Prussian-German militarism, as we have already shown, both good and evil are certainly to be distinguished from one another. Boyen, a student of Kant and of Scharnhorst, was not only a soldier who wanted a large and effective army, but also an educator of the people in political ethics. Through universal military service he wanted to give a higher moral content to service in war and to the life of the nation, just as one implants a nobler strain by the process of grafting. With his ideal of a militia for defense he fought against the cruder militarism which came from Frederick William I. Boyen's militarism was certainly not lacking in ethical values. But by its spiritual narrowness it lost touch with higher cultural values, and then, when regarded merely as the state's agency for power, helped to evoke the mad craze for power of the later nineteenth century. In these struggles of Boyen, which I had to describe, I became aware for the first time of the two-fold nature of the Prussian soul. A higher and a lower principle were always struggling with one another, and the lower principle won. This we must today quite honestly admit to ourselves, and draw our conclusions from it. The lower and degenerate militarism, which could blindly become the tool of a Hitler and which finally reached its last vicious peak in Himmler's *Waffen*-SS, is hopeless. It can, indeed it must, disappear in order to purify of bad germs a soil in which a future and nobler conception of self-defense can take root. For in Central Europe no nation without a sound conception of self-defense can in the long run live and maintain itself as a nation.

Certainly countless brave soldiers in Germany possessed such a sound idea of defense in the last war and tried to do their duty under the hardest circumstances. They are now faced with the equally hard task of struggling to realize that their idea of defense was outrageously misused and that in order to prevent a similar misuse again the former militarism must come to an end. That will be unspeakably painful, especially for those men in the officer corps who carry in themselves the nobler traditions of the Scharnhorst period. In cutting loose from the old traditions which embody much fame and pride, they lose something which to them means home and the breath of life. But have we all not lost something of home today? Let us be deeply conscious of the pain, but not allow it to oppress us, nor obscure our insight into the inevitable, nor weaken our will to life and to revival.

To be defenseless now does not mean that we shall always be defenseless. It is humiliating enough for us that when we may enjoy the rights of a free nation depends on the decision of foreign powers. Today, however, the anger over our humiliation should be turned primarily against those who are to blame for it, against the overweening pride of those who led us to the abyss, and against the lack of judgment of those who subjected themselves to this leadership without any inner protest.

The radical break with our military past that we must now accept faces us with the question about what is to become of our historical traditions in general. It would be impossible and suicidal to throw them wholesale into the fire and behave as apostates. But our customary picture of the history under which we grew to greatness needs at any rate a fundamental revision in order to discriminate between what was valuable and what was valueless. To do this, according to our conviction, only that type of historical thinking is adequate which perceives the close demonic connection between the valuable and the valueless in history. To "the eternal, iron, great laws" of our existence, of which Goethe spoke in his ode *Das Göttliche*, belongs, we believe, our impression that good and bad, divine and demonic, so often seem to grow into one another. Goethe said in the ode: "Man alone is capable of the impossible. He discriminates, chooses, judges." How the apparently impossible nevertheless becomes possible, how we in our observation so often see good and evil growing into one another and in our moral actions are able to discriminate and work for the good — that can never be fully comprehended through logic, but must be experienced in life in order to be understood. If then observation ventures the task of discriminating between the good and the bad, between the higher and the lower in our historical past and of replacing traditional accounts of the past by new evaluations, then the observer must remain aware that he is dealing with the work of mortal man and that he is bound by the momentary spirit of the age. And yet the venture must be made! Made with a sense of responsibility, with a pure, humane, and patriotic feeling.

With such a feeling we now reply to an assertion often made in the camp of the victors, namely, that the harm to the world did not originate for the first time from the Third Reich, but is much older and is derived from Bismarck, yes, from Frederick the Great. Yet both these men did not cause the world more unrest than a vigorous, upward-striving young state must naturally cause its rival neighbors. These neighbors had already had to endure plenty of wars caused by power politics and certainly could not be pleased over the

new unrest caused by a Frederick or a Bismarck. These conflicts, however, remained within the frontiers and bounds of
Old Europe, and did not threaten its culture. Or shall Prussian militarism be reproached on the basis of the criticism
which we ourselves have made of it, namely, that it brought
an element injurious to culture into Occidental development? Then perhaps Boyen's defense law of 1814, with its
universal military service which one state after another intro-
duced, would fall under this accusation. It shall not at all be
denied that in universal military service a demonic germ lies
hidden which we formerly overlooked, but which has been
revealed to us by the excesses of the First World War and
now very clearly by the fearful misuse that was made of the
military service in the Second World War. All this belongs
to the severe fundamental experience of our epoch that all
history is at the same time tragedy. The essence of tragedy
consists above all else in the fact that the divine and the
demonic in man are indissolubly linked together — as one
may read in Alfred Weber's book on the tragic element in
history.

Frederick the Great and Bismarck not only built up but
also tore down. In the criticism made by Constantin Frantz
about 1866 there lies, as we saw above, an element of truth.
At present, of course, it is easier for the thoughtful historian
to grasp such vital connections between building up and
tearing down and not forget one in thinking of the other.
But the emotional-minded layman is only too inclined to fall
from one extreme into another and to burn today what he
adored yesterday. Here we see the high mission of German
historical writing for the future: to give evidence of both
love and severity for our past and to proceed to the task of
maintaining what was truly good in it, recognizing what was
valueless, and taking warning from it when one has to take
action.

Even a partitioned Germany robbed of her national political existence, which is our lot today, ought to remember with
sorrowful mourning the unity and strength that she pre-

viously enjoyed. Her former striving for unity and strength was not merely, as Burckhardt saw it in his *Reflections on History*, a blind striving of the masses to whom culture meant nothing. Rather was it borne along, as Burckhardt was not quite fully able to understand, by that great idea of an inner union of spirit and power, by humanity and nationality. Great cultural values emerged for us from it. But this union, as we must make clear to ourselves, was disrupted through our own fault. Now the question arises, shall we immediately work for it anew? In the first place, we are at present prevented from doing so by the external control by foreign powers. To attempt at present to win back a part of the strength of such a union would today lead only to impotent convulsions. For inner reasons also, it must be renounced at present. Our conception of power must first be purified from the filth which came into it during the Third Reich before it can again be capable of forming a union with spirit and culture. The purpose of power must be reflected upon and wisely limited. The desire to become a world power has proven to be a false idol for us. Our geopolitical and geophysical situation alone forbids it. To be a world power is furthermore an adventure which cuts in two directions leading to temptations in which culture is too much the loser.

People may protest to us saying: But did not our now-shattered former world policy have a positive sense in that it furnished a livelihood for our mightily increased population? And now is it not to be feared that our eastern provinces, on whose agricultural produce we depended, will be completely lost and that there will be a severe shrinkage of our industry from which our working classes gained their livelihood. In this respect anxieties of the very darkest sort press upon us. One may indeed reproach our former world policy and the sudden striving of the Third Reich for world power with the fact that they pursued the correct aim of assuring Germany's food supply for the future but used false and finally utterly false methods. As a result, we are now brought to the lamentable situation of having our physical existence depend solely upon the insight and wisdom of the victors.

For us power has hitherto been too much of an end in itself, and furthermore, not merely for ourselves alone, but for nationalism in general. Power, however, can justify itself, outside the service that it performs for a people's needs of life, just by the service that it renders to the highest spiritual and ethical values — to culture and religion. That it is otherwise in reality and that the power of the state ever and again acts and behaves as an end in itself, the historian knows very well. But it behooves him after every necessary look at reality to lift his gaze again to mankind's highest stars. Tragic will appear the contrast that he perceives between the reality and the ideal. Tragic indeed is the history that he will have to write.

The historian has only to write down and evaluate the course of events, and not to take part in determining them. But times of great crisis lead him beyond this mission. Therefore let us state our view of the part that power is to play in our future existence, an existence which at present is so powerless. We can win back power only as a member of a future federation, voluntarily concluded, of the central and west European states. Such a United Nations of Europe will naturally accept the hegemony of the victor powers.

The time has not yet come to consider more closely the problems that will grow out of such a federation. But a look at our small Germanic neighboring peoples can teach us some lessons. Sweden and Holland were once great European powers and Switzerland at the beginning of the sixteenth century carried on a policy something like that of a great power. Today they have enough power so that if attacked they could fight manfully. Their defense spirit has remained sound and alive. They would be able to maintain themselves successfully in such a fight, to be sure, only by leaning upon at least one of the great powers. That also will be our destiny in the future.

We have therefore come into the position of these three

peoples, of being like burnt-out craters of great power politics, and yet of feeling within ourselves the appeal to remain brave and capable of self-defense. These three peoples have also given evidence of an inner vitality in their whole cultural life. They do not suffer more, or more severely, than we under the problems of the modern age, when the spontaneous spiritual creative power of the individual has to struggle against the pressure of the masses and the flattening effects of technology. All three in recent generations have given us the most beautiful and peculiarly irreplaceable fruits of their poetry, science, and art. I will name only in my own field of science the three names of Jakob Burckhardt, Huizinga, and Kjellén. No one of these three nations — Sweden, Holland, Switzerland — has forgotten the days in which it fought its battles. Each honors and loves its former heroes, even when today there is no place for heroism of the same kind. Such an existence as these three peoples live today is more for them than a kind old-age allotment apportioned to aged peasant parents. All the moral forces and energies of man find room for expression. Let us resolve to follow their example.

On the basis of what we have already said, we shall be asked: How about that intermingling of the great tendencies of the age, the two waves of the nationalist and socialist movements? We reply that the intermingling cannot be a matter of conscious rational planning, but can only proceed by a gradual evolution and in a particular manner for each people. In England, for example, the existence, attitude, and success of the Labor party today proves that it is possible to combine a strong national feeling with a strong socialistic resolve. The reason that Hitler's National Socialist experiment was so unsound was that it threw into the mixing pot the national element only in its most frightful form of a degenerate and unbridled nationalism and a racial madness. As a result, the socialist element that was thrown in from the other side was denatured and robbed of its best content. To be socialist and socialist-minded today and to act accordingly means nothing else but the following of a general humane ideal. It means applying the concept of humanity in a concrete way in modern society — and this humanity is to benefit not only one's own country but also the human community in general. To be socially and humanely minded is one and the same thing at the present stage of Occidental development, when the increased masses of the population admonish us to be so. Then, when a truly healthy intermingling of the nationalist and socialist movements has come about, it must again free us from nationalist excesses and humanize us. *Ritornar al segno* is the watchword for us and for *all* the peoples of the Occident! Did not Herder, when he arose to create a new epoch, proclaim both humanity and nationality?

Pious wishes for the future! Will they be fulfilled? We do not know. The intermingling of the two waves of our age that we foresee may again take on other and worse forms. Our task as a people, however, can at present be only to work under the auspices of humanity for the purification and intensification of our moral existence. Our houses have been destroyed and our sources of food have been curtailed. But abodes and food for the German spirit were also lacking under the Third Reich. To recover again this spirit ought at least to be just as important as the construction of houses and the production of food.

The areas in which we must spiritually establish ourselves again are marked out for us. These areas are the religion and the culture of the German people. The religious feeling arising from the need to find an anchor-hold in misfortune will presumably stir us more strongly, we hope, than after the First World War, because every other hold has become much more questionable for us than formerly. The Catholic church and the Protestant "Confessional" church are already equipping themselves with their means for reaching the hearts of men. Catholics can again attend their Corpus Christi Day processions. In the Franconian village where I lived after the war the inhabitants were celebrating the name-day of their local patron saint. The old church was richly decorated with flowers, the villagers crowded into it, and upon the peasant's hard day's work there fell again a ray from above. The Confessional church has more difficulty in becoming a popular movement because the faithful who first gathered around it were a small group.

The attitude which the victors who now rule us take toward these religious stirrings is significant. The American local commander in my district turned with preference in all small questions to the local Catholic priest. From the parts of Germany ruled by the Russians I am informed that a particularly active Confessional church pastor was granted the ration supplement given to those who do the heaviest work and that the pastors in general enjoy relatively good food rations. We know why that happens, and we should follow further the paths to which our own most essential need points.

In order, however, that this turning again to the altars of our fathers shall not become merely a return to the past and even to a renewal of the old confessional hatreds, something new must be added as the fruit of our common oppression under the heathenism of the Third Reich. This oppression affected the whole common religious possession of everything which had grown up in the course of a thousand years on the soil of the Occidental Christian community of peoples. The oppression affected the Freemasons, as we saw, no less than the Catholic church. Is there not an inner common heritage in all these religious groups that once upon a time fought one another? This common heritage is now clear in general outline. It means belief in the holy fountain of good; respect for the eternal and absolute; complete acceptance of what the devout Christian understands by Child of God; recognition of the conscience as the "sun of our moral day"; the rising above the sensual substructure of human nature; and recognition of a moral law derived from the Eternal and far above blood and race.

A deeper analysis would disclose still finer traits in this Christian common heritage. That it exists is a beautiful fact. To try to distill out a new common religion of the future would be foolish. The abundance of what is individual in the heritage would thereby be lost. To create and maintain this abundance and to let it become intermingled and grow to higher forms is part of the essence of historical life. Manifold are the roads to God, and this manifoldness should be respected. We ask from one another not merely tolerance, but respect for all the churches, creeds, sects, and religious movements which have a share in the common religious heritage of the Christian Occident. Between the Catholic and the Confessional churches a mutual respect of this kind began to develop during the years of oppression. It was not so much the content as the positive character of their teachings, the same need for a firm and immovable foundation for dogma, that brought them nearer together. It will be harder for them than for us freer and more emancipated thinkers to develop that inner respect for a really religious movement, whether it be dogmatic or undogmatic. For us this respect will have become in itself a religion — a reverence for the manifoldness of the roads that lead to God. Our particular road does not hinder us, rather it impels us to long for a still higher all-Christian community. An ecumenical Christianity could arise which clearly distinguishes itself from heathendom, and especially from the most modern heathendom of racialism. It would distinguish itself simply by knowing itself to be in historical continuity with the life, teachings, and sacrificial death of Jesus. It is to be hoped then that these two most compact Christian organizations, the Catholic and the Confessional churches, will further maintain their claims to a positive attitude. It suits their nature and should be respected. Nothing further will be hoped or wished for from them than that they tolerate the Christian inheritance of all the other communities who share in the common heritage and that they prize more highly what we have in common than what divides us. We are all in common danger and need! And our German need is in this case the need of the Christian Occident in general. For everywhere religious life is in danger of becoming dried up by modern civilization. Everything that can now stir religious life on a Christian basis helps at the same time to bridge the cleavages between peoples and to reconcile the vanquished and the victors.

We are therefore not alarmed at the prospect of seeing Protestantism work, in the future as in the past, not as a unity bound together by dogma, but as a bundle of varying religious movements. It is clearly impossible to bring about a unity without depriving countless religious persons of their home in a church. Here also the thing to do is to change from the unitary state ideal to a federal solution. Such a federation — so fraudulent an establishment, for example, as the Nazi "German Christians" of course excludes itself — would willingly embrace a new creation so forceful and vital as the Christian community founded by Rittelmeyer in 1922. Though people may perhaps treat the splitting up of churches in the United States as a sociological phenomenon, they cannot deny that genuine religious forces have released themselves through it and have combined to help build the total spirit of Americanism.

Everything, yes everything, depends upon an intensified development of our inner existence. We named the culture of the German spirit as the second of the two areas in which this must proceed. The work of Bismarck's era has been destroyed through our own fault, and we must go back beyond its ruins to seek out the ways of Goethe's era. The heights of the Goethe period and of the highly gifted generation living in it were reached by many individual men, bound together merely in small circles by ties of friendship. They strove for and to a large degree realized the ideal of a personal and wholly individual culture. This culture was thought of as having at the same time a universal human meaning and content. The religious revival that we desire is in its deepest foundation an affair of the individual human soul thirsting for a healthy recovery. It seeks strongly the formation of communities, because most people get a feeling of security and safety only by being linked together in a local religious community as part of a wider church organization. This means a great measure of organization and coöperation. But all organizations always tread upon the rank and file and sacrifice or curtail part of the individual's own inclination. But does organization alone promote spiritual culture? Does not spiritual culture demand a sphere for individual inclination, for solitude, and for the deepening of one's self?

Doubts about the certain value of organization begin in connection with the upper schools and the examination system in Germany, where so much that is external comes into play and what is inward may be injured. In Goethe's day the external things retreated very much into the background, so the inward things could develop more freely. We cannot imitate that; we stand too much under the pressure of everything that the external has meanwhile created and organized around us. In order to keep our striving for inner development free from the pressure of these organizations, we must ourselves, paradoxically enough, occasionally turn to organizing. To what a high degree today, for instance, is the arrangement of concerts organized. The daily life of the artist is swept into a whirlpool of modern activity, whereas in the palace and house music of Goethe's day there was much more freedom, unconstraint, and truly individual spontaneity.

Therefore our spiritual culture, especially our art, poetry, and science, must be assigned a high place in the external apparatus of our civilization. Today in Germany this apparatus lies in ruins. It is impossible to restore it as it was. Perhaps a restoration in every respect is not necessary. It would be much better if the German spirit could grow up again so free, so personal, so spontaneous and unconstrained as formerly, and need no hot-house forcing. Nevertheless, today some organizational assistance is needed in order to afford the first nourishment to those hungering and thirsting after beauty and the spirit.

To know that many places in Germany are already stirring with efforts of this kind is one of the very few experiences of our time which can give us immediate comfort. One hears of culture leagues and culture communities in the cities. One hears of theatrical productions in which the treasures of German drama are again rising into the light. Young men and old crowd to concerts in which the great old German music is played. But here and there the immediate purpose of these cultural activities is proclaimed to be the denazifying of the German spirit. Let us not speak too much of this purpose. Let us not take too ponderously as an objective what we most urgently desire. Just as there ought not to be too much organization in this field, the purposeful aspect and matters which border on the political sphere must be handled with tact and moderation. Spiritual life and the striving for spiritual values are their own justification and work most deeply where their movements can be most free from political tendencies. Indeed they work most deeply and beneficially by themselves when they go their own ways spontaneously and unregulated.

We desire therefore that these cultural strivings of ours shall have as free and unconstrained a treatment as possible. Thereby something further will be reached, which is also urgently to be desired but which must not be pushed too obviously and consciously: namely, the winning back of a spiritual contact with the other Occidental countries. For it is a fact that precisely the cultivation of our own peculiarly individual German spiritual life is what can bind us in the purest and most natural way with the spiritual life of other nations. What is more individual and German than the great German music from Bach to Brahms? It was precisely this that was taken up most thankfully by the rest of the world and brought us spiritually nearer to it. In comparison with the universal effect which our music as a whole has been able to exert, the other fields of our cultural life — art, poetry, science — have exerted their effect only in the case of single great achievements. But it has always been a fact that a specifically and genuinely German spiritual production has succeeded in having a universal Occidental effect. What is more German than Goethe's *Faust* and how powerfully has it cast its radiance upon the Occident! Whatever springs from the very special spirit of a particular people and is therefore inimitable is likely to make a successful universal appeal. This fact is not limited in its application only to the relation of the German to the Occidental spirit. It also illustrates a fundamental law of the Occidental cultural community in general. We just mention it, but it could be more thoroughly demonstrated than is possible here. What is more Italian than Raphael's Madonna della Sedia, and what a magic spell it casts at the same time on every sensitive cultured Occidental person! How deeply are Shakespeare's plays rooted in English soil, and yet how tremendously they have shaken and permeated the whole Occident! In order to exert a universal influence, spiritual possessions of this kind must always blossom forth naturally, uniquely, and organically out of any given folk spirit. They must originate free, spontaneous, purposeless, from the most inner creative impulse. So as soon as there stirs the vain purpose of demonstrating to the rest of the Occident the superiority of one's own folk spirit, imitating the racial madness of the Third Reich, its influence on the Occident is nil and other peoples reject it with scorn.

Four decades ago, in the field of political history, I tried to show that cosmopolitanism and the modern idea of the national state were not originally rigid contrasts, but existed together for mutual enrichment or, as one might say after the fashion of Goethe and Hegel, in a polar and dialectical tension and connection with one another. Today, after a generation of the most tremendous revolutions, let us recognize that for Occidental cultural life a similar dialectic is applicable. Here also cosmopolitanism and national feelings are not rigid contrasts but are interwoven with one another. The cosmopolitan cultural community of the Christian Occident, as it has actually existed and as according to our most ardent wishes it should now again blossom forth, did not originate only from superimposed and essentially universal ideas and ideals, but also from quite individual and inimitable contributions of individual folk spirits. The most universal and the most individualistic can here be married to one another. Is that not a rich comfort for us in our present tragic situation? We do not need any radical change in schooling in order to function effectively again in the Occidental cultural community. But the Nazi megalomania with its unculture and afterculture must absolutely disappear. Its place does not have to be taken by pale, empty, abstract cosmopolitanism, but by a cosmopolitanism which in the past was formed by the coöperation of the most individual German contributions and which is to be further formed in the future. The German spirit, we hope and believe, after it has found itself again, has still to fulfill its special and irreplaceable mission within the Occidental community.

I should like in conclusion to sketch a little wishful picture which came into my mind in the frightful weeks after the collapse. It touches those tendencies, which have meanwhile achieved success, for the cultivation of our cultural life that I have already mentioned. Among the favorable experiences upon which we can draw are some that come even from the Third Reich. The sly Goebbels knew very precisely, for example, how one could snare harmless souls by putting a couple of good articles worth their price in the show window of the Nazi party. Every Sunday morning at church time when he wanted to keep people from attending service he offered them on the radio a little "Treasure Chest" that gave the most beautiful German music and choice poetical pieces to those who listened in. I heard how, not long before the collapse, old Friedrich Kayssler instituted a Goethe afternoon in the Harnack House in Dahlem and recited Goethe's poetry to a small but unusually sensitively inclined circle of hearers. My thoughts finally went back to the Greeks and how their Homer sank at first into their hearts much more through the rhapsodies to which they listened than through reading. We have today many opportunities for cultivating the art of recitation and for reminding men that poetry at its birth was adapted to the living sound of the spoken word and not to the printed page.

In every German city and larger village, therefore, we should like to see in the future a community of like-minded friends of culture which I should like best to call Goethe Communities. It may be objected that the name will be interpreted as non-permissible competition with the long-existing Goethe Society in Weimar and its numerous local groups. I hope not because the tasks are different and there ought not to be a Goethe monopoly. I could imagine and wish, in fact, not an organizational but a humanly close and stimulating relationship between the members of the Goethe Society and the Goethe Communities.

To the Goethe Communities would fall the task of conveying into the heart of the listeners through sound the most vital evidences of the great German spirit, always offering the noblest music and poetry together. One need, the lack of books, into which we fell through the burning of so many libraries, bookstores, and publishing houses supports this proposal. Who today is in complete possession even of his favorite books, his complete Goethe, Schiller, and so forth? Many young men may perhaps in the future have their first access to the imperishable poems of Hölderlin, Mörike, C. F. Meyer, and Rilke at one of those regular music and poetry festal hours of the Goethe Communities which we desire as a permanent institution everywhere among us — perhaps weekly at a late Sunday afternoon hour, and if at all possible in a church! The religious basis of our poetry justifies, yes demands, its being made clear by a symbolic procedure of this kind. The beginning and close of such a festal hour might be elevated by great German music — by Bach, Mozart, Beethoven, Schubert, Brahms, and so forth.

Lyrical and thoughtful poetry could then form the kernel of such festal hours. Lyrics of the wonderful sort, reaching their peak in Goethe and Mörike where the soul becomes nature and nature the soul, and sensitive, thoughtful poetry like that of Goethe and Schiller — these are perhaps the most essentially German parts of our literature. He who steeps himself in them will detect something indestructible — a German *character indelebis* — in the midst of all the destruction and misfortune of our Fatherland.

Besides poems, anthologies of German prose must also be read in these festal hours. There might be a *Handbook for Goethe Communities* indicating the right prose, with suggestions for programs for special festal hours and with all kinds of organizational hints. I shall not sketch this further here, in order not to anticipate the free creative activity of individuals. The whole idea must start with individuals, personalities, the special few who first build among themselves only one such Goethe Community, and then let it develop here in one form, there in another.

The German state is crushed, and wide lands are lost to us. Rule by foreigners is our destiny for a long time. Shall we succeed in saving the German spirit? Never in its history has this spirit had to endure such a severe test. Historical examples of success or failure do not help us very much here. The task each time is a new and individual one. Deep faith and anxious care must help us in our attempts to solve it. Then let us look up to the highest spheres of the Eternal and Divine from whence resound for us the words: "We bid you to hope."